HELPING YOURSELF WITH AUTOGENICS

Sidney Petrie
in association with
Robert B. Stone, Ph.D.

Parker Publishing Company, Inc. West Nyack, N.Y.

This book is a reference work based on research by the author. The opinions expressed herein are not necessarily those of, or endorsed by, the publisher. The directions stated in this book are in no way to be considered as a substitute for consultation with a duly licensed doctor.

Library of Congress Cataloging in Publication Data

Petrie, Sidney.
Helping yourself with autogenics.

Includes index.
1. Autogenic training. 2. Mental health.
I. Stone, Robert B. II. Title.
RC499.A8P49 1983 158'.1 82-14488
ISBN 0-13-387407-9
ISBN 0-13-387399-4 {PBK}

Printed in the United States of America

What This Book Can Do For You

LET ME INTRODUCE MYSELF. My name is Sidney Petrie, founder of The Petrie Method® which, through the New York Institute for Hypnotherapy, has helped thousands to control their lives naturally and effortlessly through hypnotic techniques.

Now let me introduce somebody else: Dr. Johannes H. Schultz. In the early part of this century, he was the founder of Autogenic Training which helped thousands in his native Germany and throughout Europe to control their lives naturally and effortlessly through hypnotic techniques.

Yes, the late Dr. Schultz and I have at least a little in common. It is the pooling of this common ground that has given birth to Autogenics, a simple, fast way that anybody, young or old can use to change his or her life. It is a self-hypnotic technique which you can use in just a few minutes of practice to improve your health, behavior, personality and social relationships, and which can lead you to financial success.

Autogenics, this birthchild of the Petrie Method® and Autogenic Training, puts the reins in your hands. You do not need a trainer or a hypnotist. All you need is this book. It is the "recipe" book for the rest of your life.

Great meals do not happen in the kitchen by merely reading the recipe book. You have to put the book down and do something. It is the same with the book you have in your hands. In order to create a great new life for yourself, you have to stop reading, put the book down and do something.

What you do is so simple it makes cooking seem complicated by comparison and what you do is so quickly accomplished, it makes kitchen work tedious by contrast. All you do is three things: 1. create a peaceful mood (I'll tell you an easy way to do this); 2. relax your body (there are fun ways to do this); 3. affirm the change you wish to take place in your life.

When you affirm in the autogenics way that you want to get rid of stress, pain, anxiety, tension and pressure—they go.

When you affirm that you want to get rid of pesky functional disease symptoms—the problems disappear.

When you affirm that you want to change from guilt feelings, useless worry, and depression to peace of mind, confidence and enthusiasm—you do.

When you affirm that you want to take control of habits, attitudes, situations, love relationships, and career progress—you are successful.

These are not idle promises. If they were, my work would be confined to the one office in Great Neck, Long Island, that I opened some 25 years ago. It is not. It has been necessary to open offices in all the five boroughs of New York City, in Westchester, and as far south as Atlanta.

I have written a number of books on hypnotism, self-hypnotism, mental isometrics, and hypno-cybernetics that have enabled their readers to hopefully work some wonders in their lives. But Autogenics takes the best of this and, with the help of Dr. Schultz' approach, places in your hands a very powerful tool for self-help.

All you basically need is a comfortable chair and this book. You may also want to use a piece of black paper the size and shape of a quarter, a piece of string and a button, a flashlight, and a hand mirror. For some of the changes spelled out in this book, you will need another person to read certain passages to you or you can make a cassette tape of your voice.

It is recommended, even though you may not have any health problems, that you still read the first three chapters and get comfortable with the three steps: setting the mood, inducing relaxation, and affirming the change—such as going from good health to even better health.

I call these three steps, *formulae*. Each formula is single and quick in its results. Each chapter has a different cluster of advantages you can gain. After the first three chapters, you can pick and choose or you can claim them all:

- An alleviation of constipation, allergy, insomnia, headaches, and similar health problems

- Relief from some of the symptoms of arthritis, colitis, asthma, diabetes and other distress
- The end of stress from office or family or environment and of fears and phobias of all kinds
- Control over emotions, sexual pleasure, and moods
- Substituting peace of mind for anxiety, indecision and confusion
- Ending overeating, smoking and other unwanted habits
- Changing personality traits that hold you back
- Breaking out of financial ruts and moving into new levels of financial prosperity
- Setting new goals for a great new life and reaching them

Are you ready to claim some of these benefits for yourself now? Fine—let's move ahead together.

Sidney Petrie

Other Books by the Authors

The Wonder Protein Diet: Miracle Way to Better Health and Longer Life

Fat Destroyer Foods: The Magic Metabolizer Diet

Hypno-Cybernetics: Helping Yourself to a Rich New Life

TABLE OF CONTENTS

7. How to Lose Weight Without Will Power *(cont.)*

8. How to Stop Smoking and Other Unwanted Habits ...129

9. How to Improve Skills and Abilities 144

10. Autogenics for Solving Daily Problems 157

CHAPTER 1

Autogenics: What It Is and How It Works for You

A MAN IS SEATED in an arm chair in his living room. His eyes are closed, yet he is awake and alert—listening. A voice is speaking. It does not come from the television set. The radio is off. It is coming from a cassette player. He is listening to his own voice.

His own voice is telling him how to relax. As he listens, he enters a serene, tranquil state. Now his own voice is telling him how to increase his income. It is telling him about his own productivity and ability. In about 15 minutes, his voice ends the relaxation session. He opens his eyes. Within weeks this man has started a private business that does not interfere with his job. He is successful and his income doubles.

A woman is seated on a couch. Her daughter is seated opposite her and is reading from this book. The woman relaxes and following her daughter's instructions, pictures herself slender, free of the excess pounds that are interfering with her energy and health. Within a month she has lost 20 pounds and feels years younger.

A young lady is seated in her studio apartment. She is holding a hand mirror. She is relaxed, seeing herself attractive, free of skin blemishes, radiant, and accompanied by an attractive male. Within weeks she is engaged to be married.

The man, the woman, and the young lady have been applying Autogenics. It is a hypnotic technique that anybody can use to improve health, accomplishments, and the quality of his or her life.

Some 20 years ago, hypnosis was clouded by an aura of mysticism. But then the British Medical Association and the American Medical Association lifted the Svengali mask and gave hypnotism their stamp of approval as a safe and effective therapy. Now, people from all walks of life are benefiting from hypnotic techniques, not only in the United States, but around the world.

The work of many devoted researchers brought about this change. One, Dr. Johannes H. Schultz, founded Autogenic Training in Germany. He helped to make hypnotism respectable among his early 20th century contemporaries by the effectiveness of the method in helping people to overcome unwanted habits, personality quirks, fears and phobias, and a host of physical ailments.

When I began my practice as a clinical hypnologist a quarter of a century ago, I had at my disposal not only the successful techniques worked out by Dr. Schultz, but also a variety of approaches of other researchers who had made names for themselves by helping people to help themselves.

I have worked to attempt to simplify these methods so that everybody who uses them can be successful. Over a half-million therapy hours later, conducted personally or under my supervision, a system has emerged which is probably the easiest, fastest and most inexpensive way available to you to break out of ruts caused by nagging health problems, limited finances, or personal idiosyncracies and into a bright new world of renewed youth, heightened vigor, enhanced skills, and happier days.

I call the method Autogenics.

How the Power of Autogenics Can Give You a Rich New Life Almost Immediately

Look around you. Some people fail. Others succeed. Some win love and blossom forth in life. Others are lonely and wither on the vine. Yet, the losers and the winners are playing the same game, under the same rules and with the same equipment. What, then, spells the difference?

The answer is: your mind.

Your mind controls your body. Your mind controls your skills. Your mind controls your relationships with other people.

Can you imagine the kind of life you would lead if you were in control of your mind!

If you follow the instructions in the first three chapters of this book, you can attain that control. You will then be able to exercise that control in whatever department of your life that you wish to "blossom."

Yes, you can gain relief from common ailments and even more serious health problems. But what is probably more important, you can use Autogenics to help you solve those daily problems that seem to interfere with smooth sailing. You can use it to cope with those impossible damned-if-you-do, damned-if-you-don't situations and apparently insoluble problems.

Yes, you can use Autogenics to lose weight, stop smoking, cut down on drinking, and to get rid of other unwanted modes of behavior. But what is just as important, you can use Autogenics to improve your skills, increase your personal assets, gain protection from stress, and attain peace of mind.

It is all so simple and so fast that it is a wonder it is not required training in every school. Pilot projects are currently underway in a number of educational institutions, so hopefully, one day, people everywhere will know that they are in control of their lives and can move in any direction they wish.

Meanwhile, why wait? Declare your independence from all past worries, problems, and limitations. Take charge of your life.

When you began to read this chapter, you took the first step. As you read further, you will learn that the two basic ingredients for control are (1) relaxation and (2) visualization. As you put the book down and follow the simple directions, you will acquire easy step-by-step procedures for enjoying deep relaxation and for using the imaging faculty of your mind to activate the fantastic three-pound organ we call the brain.

David is tall and distinguished-looking. He and his two brothers were in the import-export business, each brother having a specific duty. During the past year, tragedy had struck David's family. One brother died of a sudden heart attack. Five weeks later, his other brother suffered a mild stroke. Although he had returned to work, it was on a limited scale.

David now had to manage the entire business—traveling, buying, selling, managing, hiring—tasks that were formerly shared by his two brothers. In desperation he hired assistants. This complicated things even further because now there had to be time put aside for training. David, the oldest of the three brothers, was now convinced that he was pushing himself into an early grave. He came to our New York Institute for Hypnotherapy as a last resort.

We decided that David's priority must be to do one thing at a time. He responded very well to that target and some weeks later reported that he felt strong, healthy and, most of the time, relaxed. Using Autogenics to relax and to promote this ability to be focused in his activities, David began to emerge from his business dilemma. He developed a new attitude toward living and though he worked harder than ever before, he appreciated his free time off. He also reported that although he was working under even greater pressure than ever, he was handling it better than he had ever dealt with it before. Instead of cracking under the pressure, he felt that he was thriving on it.

Notice the use of the word "target" in this case. Many problems appear to be complicated. But there is usually one element of the problem which is critical. Handle this element, or target, and the knotty problem unravels.

If you were to ask me whether a certain problem you have in your life could be helped with Autogenics, I would be ready to answer "yes" long before you finished describing all of the complex interrelated details of the problem.

This does not make Autogenics some kind of miraculous approach. Autogenics merely utilizes the miraculous abilities of the human brain.

How Autogenics Triggers Your Mind to Do Super-Work for You

When Johannes H. Schultz, the Berlin psychiatrist and neurologist who founded Autogenic Training, first became interested in this field, it was a direct result of the work in the late 1800's done by O. Vogt and K. Brodmann at the Berlin Neuro-Biological Institute. They discovered that patients could be taught to put themselves into a state similar to hypnosis—autohypnosis and that in this state their minds obeyed their orders to recuperate from whatever ailed them.

Dr. Schultz was strongly motivated to help people help themselves,—to become less dependent on the therapist, in this case the hypnotist. By observing certain common characteristics of hypnotized patients, he developed a simple procedure enabling anybody to induce a hypnotic state. These common characteristics included a relaxed, casual attitude of non-striving, non-trying. So he developed a simple way to set this mood.

These common characteristics also included feelings of heaviness and of warmth in the arms and legs. So he encouraged these feelings as a simple way for anybody to induce the hypnotic state on his own.

My work has paralleled that of Dr. Schultz. And although it involves new techniques to extend the abilities acquired through Autogenic Training, it is still based on Dr. Schultz's techniques.

What Dr. Schultz could not possibly understand in his day was what we now know about the tremendous capabilities of the human brain unleashed by these techniques.

Computers were unknown in his day. To say then that the brain had computer-like ability would not have any meaning. But we know this to be so today. We know that each of the brain's 30 billion neurons is like a component of a computer. Even with miniaturized circuits, a computer with 30 billion components would probably be as big as the Empire State Building, if we indeed had the resources to build it.

You have such a super-computer. Whether you are 30 years old, or 40, or 50, or 60, you have never put it to full use. In fact, you have used only a tiny fraction of its vast intelligence.

By inducing a hypnotic state through Autogenics, you are taking the cover off this wondrous computer and exposing all the buttons. All you have to do then is to push the right buttons. Then those 30 billion neurons, all in touch with each other through trillions of connecting circuits, come up with answers.

What kind of answers? The answers delivered by your brain do not come by "read out" as a computer might deliver them on a strip of paper. They come by "behave out."

You behave differently. Here are some examples of this different behavior. You can order any of these yourself and get quick action:

- End energy-sapping headaches
- Relieve chronic pain as from arthritis or rheumatism
- Ease cold symptoms
- Improve complexion
- Overcome nausea
- Get rid of constipation
- End insomnia
- Facilitate putting on contact lens
- Relieve allergies such as hay fever
- Help with dental problems
- Decrease asthma attacks
- Eliminate oversensitive gas reflexes
- Diminish gastro-intestinal disorders
- Decrease menstrual distress
- End self-consciousness, or fear of performing
- Get rid of fear of heights, of crowds, of water, of the dark, of closed spaces
- Handle frigidity, impotence, homosexuality
- End anxiety, insecurity or inferiority
- Become decisive
- Change instability
- Go from boredom to enthusiasm, impatience to patience, doubt to assuredness
- Lose weight effortlessly and permanently
- Stop smoking, coffee drinking, excessive drinking
- Halt nail-biting, bed-wetting, hair-twisting
- Play better bridge or a musical instrument
- Be a better golfer, jogger, tennis player, bowler
- Improve typing, writing, sewing, bookkeeping
- End paralyzing grief
- Overcome personal bias
- Gain control over other people
- Transform yourself into a super-idea generator

- Release endless energy
- Win more friends and supporters
- Become a better conversationalist
- Change from a non-doer to a doer
- Replace jealousy with trust and understanding
- Acquire the habit of being successful

These are everyday changes that your brain can accomplish for you once you know how to use Autogenics—once you know how to program your wondrous computer.

A Surprising Brain Element That Even a Computer Does Not Have

The human brain has developed over the millennia by adding layers. Deep within the brain is the same brain that reptiles still have. Surrounding that core is the more advanced middle area with later mammal advances. The cortex or outer level is man's latest addition—his own special superiority.

All of these levels still work for us, from the reptilian's need for protection, sex, territory, etc.; through the mammalian's later skills and intuition, to the inductive and deductive reasoning of Homo sapiens.

There is a section of our mind in which all information, memory and experience are stored. You make decisions, react to situations, respond to emotions, all by virtue of this section of your mind, which incidentally, is in touch with all of the layers just mentioned.

This special section of your mind also informs you of your inner feelings about yourself. What you are right now, sitting and reading this page, is what your mind believes you are.

Did you spill your milk as a child and did an authoritarian voice say to you "Clumsy!" Your mind might well have accepted that about you. If so, it can be behaving as *clumsy*. Or did you do something to annoy your mother or father or big brother and did they respond with "Stupid!" If your brain accepted that, it gave you lower marks in school and a lower success rate in life.

Your ability to succeed, to overcome a problem, to accomplish a task, to reach a goal depends largely on your mind's belief in your abilities.

When you are called on to perform in a certain way, this special section of your mind puts out a call for all pertinent information stored at all levels of the mind. It then assimilates this information and tells you whether you can or cannot perform in that way.

We are going to call this special section of your mind the Intelligence Filter. The Intelligence Filter, therefore, is that section of your mind that reports to you your beliefs.

For instance, if you ask yourself, "Could I undergo surgery without the aid of an anesthetic and be without pain?" your Intelligence Filter is the part of your mind that answers, "No."

Similarly, if you ask yourself, "Will I be successful at this new venture?" the Intelligence Filter will respond with an answer that is based on a lifetime of prior conditioning or input of how you feel about yourself.

If your belief about yourself is one of insecurity, then all answers by the Intelligence Filter will be affected by that belief.

But if that belief is changed to a more positive self-image, then the response of the Intelligence Filter will be correspondingly more positive.

Once this positive change has been effected, the Intelligence Filter will direct all stored information in your billions of brain neurons to produce the positive end result.

That is why people who say "I can't" are always correct. They really cannot, because they believe they cannot.

And that is why those who say "I can"—can.

The Limitless Mind Can Be Both Limited and Delimited

We got a call one day from a major insurance company asking us whether or not we had a methodology that could produce greater motivation amongst their sales personnel. An arrangement was made whereby we would conduct group sessions with a number of their employees. These sessions went very well. At the end of four weeks, these employees' sales were up 8 percent. By the end of the year, their sales were up 16 percent.

One man, who had been in their employ for 12 years, who had never written more than half a million dollars in a year, received an award for writing one million dollars that year.

Here is the way the group was conducted. Each member of the group was asked to write a list of what he believed prevented him from making greater sales. The listings were quite similar. In the main, they included procrastination, lack of enthusiasm, lack of attention to detail, lack of structure and lack of confidence. Each person was instructed to look at his individual list and put these areas in order of importance—the most important area was to be number one—up to the least important of these areas which needed to be overcome.

The next instructions were to choose the listing at the very bottom—the one that was the least important—and to isolate that. And that was to be their first target point. They were to accomplish that before reaching the next area.

They were told to sit comfortably in a chair at home and to establish communication with their Intelligence Filter. I will tell you how to do this in the next chapter. They were then to ask permission of their Intelligence Filter to work toward that particular goal. If there was an objection to that, they would ask their mind to investigate the cause of the problem, and to resolve it so we could get a direct pathway to the target point. Once their mind had accepted the reality of their goal, the Intelligence Filter was instructed to make the necessary changes in order to reach that goal. At a future group session, each participant then zeroed in on the next area on his list. This was continued until the whole list was covered.

Of the 20 men in the group, two claimed no benefits, 5 claimed some benefits, and 13 claimed the benefits were outstanding.

These salesmen had identified their limiting beliefs and then changed them.

Just as our fabulous mind can be programmed for limitation by certain beliefs, so can it be reprogrammed by changing these beliefs.

Sales curves can be changed. So can hip curves, thigh curves and bust curves. The mind shapes the body and you can reprogram your mind to shape a more well-proportioned body, as well as a more efficient stomach, straighter back and pain-free anatomy.

All skills, habits, personality quirks, and well-being factors respond in like manner to reprogramming. What the reprogramming does really is to eliminate limiting beliefs. Once this is done, your mind can accomplish the most difficult tasks. It can overcome the most disabling of habits or behavioral patterns. It can control pain. It can change unwanted or negative attitudes.

Your mind can do all this and much more once it is freed of limiting programming and allowed to precisely combine all information accessible to it and seek out a pathway to success.

This pathway will take directions that the mind has not taken before. New beliefs permit the mind to perform in a manner that you have not been able to perform under old beliefs and therefore to succeed in ways heretofore impossible for you.

In effect, Autogenics can then expand your abilities, extend your life, and enhance your abilities.

Can you ask for more?

The Equipment You Will Use in Autogenics

Walk into my office and you will find it quite different from a dentist's office or a doctor's office. There is no equipment that strikes the eye. It is a comfortable living room atmosphere.

That is the main requirement now for you. You need a comfortable, quiet place in which to do Autogenics. Even a living room can change from a quiet place to a noisy, frenetic place at certain times of the day. So you need to plan your Autogenics for those quiet times.

Once in your quiet living room or bedroom locale, you are going to be given about ten minutes of instructions to follow. You cannot follow them by reading. Your eyes must be closed and you must be doing with your mind what the instructions call for. So you will need to make tapes and play them back. Or you will need the services of a neighbor, friend or family member to read the few pages to you.

If you have a cassette tape player that does not record, you may need to borrow one that does. It takes just about ten minutes to make a tape of the instructions. And, of course, once you have it, you can use it over and over again as needed. All you do is turn on the tape recorder and read the few pages of instructions that will appear later in this book. You read aloud slowly at a moderate tone level, just as if you were reading aloud to a friend, only this time the friend is yourself.

Once the tape is made, all you will need to do is turn on the tape recorder and listen to the instructions you give yourself. As you follow these instructions—relaxing and thinking in the manner described—you are changing limiting beliefs and reprogramming yourself to reach the goals you have set.

Of course, if you do not have a cassette recorder and player, and cannot borrow one, you will need to enlist the help of another person. You need to explain the purposes to this person, so it should be a person you can confide in and depend on. When this person is available to you, you can hold your Autogenics session in that person's house, if different from your own, to make it more convenient for that person. All that person is asked to do is to read the few pages of instructions that help you to relax deeply and that enable you to reprogram yourself to improve in some way.

In addition to this, I will offer you ways involving some simple household objects that will help to make Autogenics even easier and more effective for you.

Let me just list these at this time so you can plan ahead, without my telling you exactly to what use these will be put. Helpful objects to have handy later will be a button, a string, a piece of paper with a black circle on it, a flashlight, and a hand mirror.

To satisfy your curiosity just a little, the button on a string will be used as a pendulum to probe the subconscious. A black circle, affixed to the wall will help with concentration, a flashlight will be used in relaxation, and a hand mirror will help with directing instructions to yourself.

More about the specific uses of these household items as we progress.

The Growing Popularity of Hypnotic Techniques

Autogenics is a hypnotic technique. This means that it entails psychophysiologic relaxation—relaxation of mind and body. The word "autogenic" means self-generated. So Autogenics is a self-generated state of relaxation used in a hypnotic way for self-improvement.

Psychophysiologic relaxation is the exact opposite of stress. When you relax by listening to the instructions, you are entering a state diametrically opposed to a stressful state.

A stressful state impedes efficiency, creates personality problems, and interferes with health.

When you enter a relaxed state, you automatically restore natural efficiency, regain personal harmony, and improve your health.

Scientists have found that white blood cell count decreases when a person is under stress. This means that stress lowers one's natural resistance to disease. It is also known that mental stress can be passed on to vital organs. Any organ under stress can eventually fail to perform in healthy ways.

Stress management is an increasingly popular skill. Stress is a killer. Stress management enables you to handle stress without paying the price. The price can not only be in years off your life, but in points off your test grades, and in dollars off your income.

Stress management involves relaxation techniques. It also involves mental programming techniques. Yes, Autogenics is stress management. It is many other things, but its use in the handling of stressful life situations has accelerated its popularity in this increasingly stressful world.

Hypnotic techniques which I use in the New York Institute of Hypnotherapy have generated increasing interest among medical practitioners in recent years. There are more and more referrals of patients by doctors in most every medical specialty.

"My heartiest congratulations on your most important and brilliant approach to solving a most difficult problem in an easy, sensible, safe and healthy technique."

It is not often that a paramedic, if I may call myself that, is so commended. The praise comes from Morris Wilkin, M.D., F.R.C.P., an authority in his field.

Another authority, noted psychiatrist, author, and lecturer Frank S. Caprio, M.D., comments on our programs, "Petrie's system of conditioning has already proven effective for thousands. Every person who has a problem could be helped enormously by this excellent method."

I repeat these words with all modesty, not for the purpose of blowing my horn, but rather to blow the horn for hypnotic techniques.

At last they have come of age. At least the fear is gone, the mystery dissolved, and the benefits acknowledged full square.

Many medical schools in the United States provide courses for both undergraduate and graduate students on hypnotic theory and techniques. We now boast two societies in the United States dedicated to clinical and experimental hypnosis: the International Society of Clinical and Experimental Hypnosis, and the American Society of Clinical Hypnosis. Their combined membership is close to 3,000. Both are recognized by the American Medical Association and the courses of instruction offered by members of their educational and research divisions are recognized for professional credit.

In the last five years there have been approximately one thousand published scientific papers dealing with hypnosis. Popular media have become increasingly interested. My own work in hypnotherapy has been covered on television by CBS, NBC, and ABC. Television stations have covered it in Boston (WBZ), New York (WOR), Washington (WTOP), Los Angeles (WPIX), Phoenix (KOOL), Las Vegas (KLAS), and even in London (BBC). Commentators such as David Susskind, Merv Griffin, and Martha Graham have interviewed me or my associates. And prestigious newspapers and magazines—the New York Times, Chicago Tribune, Los Angeles Times, Cosmopolitan, Redbook, Jet, and Woman's Day have written about our work,—a topic that was editorially taboo a few decades ago.

Autogenics and other hypnotic techniques are now an accepted part of the holistic approach to better health and a better life.

What You Actually Do in Autogenics

You will begin to use Autogenics in the next chapter. But, of course, you have no idea now of what to expect. It is an unknown process to you. Anything that is unknown is usually a threat, or frightening. Let me erase that feeling right now.

There is nothing about Autogenics that is new or strange. It merely puts together in a meaningful sequence and with a specific purpose what you have already been doing without that sequence or purpose. Here are some of the things that you have been doing which, when properly synthesized, become Autogenics.

Can you imagine the last time you sat looking at a beautiful sunset? Or watched the moon rise? Or listened to the patter of raindrops? Do you remember how you felt? These natural events set a mood. So do human events. You have undoubtedly experienced love, anger, hope, despair. In Autogenics, you begin by creating a mood. It is usually a mood of serenity and expectation of betterment.

Look at your hand as you hold this book. Notice how the fingers are positioned. Be aware of the feeling of your hand, its warmth, its heaviness, the contact of the fingers with the book. In Autogenics, you use this kind of awareness to promote a type of quietude.

Next, make yourself more comfortable in your chair or wherever you are reading. Take a deep breath and as you exhale, permit your body to relax. Forget concerns and anxieties. Know all is well. Feel peacefulness. You will learn how to do this more effectively in Autogenics.

Now, I am going to ask you to stop reading in a moment, and to daydream. Daydream about something pleasant like going on a trip or shopping for new clothing. Close your eyes for a few moments and do it now...

Finally, can you imagine yourself in those new clothes or with somebody you adore or reaching some heart's desire? Again, close your eyes for a few moments and do it now...

You have just experienced most of the kinds of things you will be doing in Autogenics. Is it to be feared? On the contrary, you should be looking forward to it, because it is familiar ground, and it is both simple and pleasant.

Rita, 36, divorced, was attending interior design school. She liked this work and felt she could support herself at it. But things were not going well in the school for her. She tensed up at every assignment. She worried whether she was absorbing the information at every lecture. Rita knew she was a failure in life because of her unsuccessful marriage. She also knew she had been out of school a long time and would have difficulty getting back into the student role. In short, Rita had already programmed herself to fail.

However, she was smart enough to know what she was doing to herself. That is why she sought help from me.

In just two or three hours, Rita learned to set a mood, relax, and think in terms of change. In her case it was a change in the direction of being more relaxed about her training and more confident in her own abilities. While relaxed, she told herself "Whatever I concentrate on, I can recall at will."

With the tension turned off, Rita found immediate results. She had plenty of time to do her assignments. She was more confident in class and did much better on exams. She later received her accreditation and became a practicing interior designer.

The Promise of Autogenics for You

Recently, scientists did time-lapse photography of a crayfish being attacked from behind. Instantly, the crayfish contracted its abdomen and then re-extended it, all the while rolling over and over. The result was a somersault that permitted the crayfish to swim away in the opposite direction. All of this complicated maneuver was accomplished in less than a half a second. It took place because a single cell in the crayfish's nervous system was stimulated.

We are billions of times more developed and complicated than the crayfish. We are constantly being attacked, too. We call such attacks "stress." These attacks come in the form of health problems, money problems, sex and marriage problems, family problems, and accomplishment problems.

Our brain neurons react to this stress, but the reaction is different from the crayfish's. We cannot turn about-face and run from the danger. We are a captive in the situation. So the brain neurons cause us to be irritable and nervous. Perhaps we lose sleep, get headaches, or take to drinking. Perhaps we have feelings of worthlessness or hostility. Perhaps we mistrust others and hate ourselves for our personal shortcomings.

We might find ourselves confused and worried. We take more time from work or school. We miss deadlines and appointments. We become forgetful. We are indecisive, even withdrawn. We lose our perspective. Problems become out of proportion and insurmountable.

Physical reactions then become inevitable. We are candidates for ulcers, migraine headaches, colitis, high blood pressure. We become accident-prone, diabetes-prone, heart disease-prone, and prone to just about every serious disease that plagues mankind, starting perhaps with overeating, overdrinking, and other such excesses which seem to be the cause. But you remember the real cause—stress.

Just the way stress touches off this tragic chain of events, so Autogenics reverses it.

You are able, in Autogenics, to give your brain neurons something different from stress to which to react. You are able to give your brain neurons a message different from attack—a message of survival.

I am going to teach you in just a few minutes of reading exactly how to give your brain neurons a stimulus for whatever corrective response you deem necessary for greater success and happiness in your life.

You will have a pleasant experience doing it, because your brain neurons are geared for survival; indeed, every cell of your body will applaud your doing it, as you change the climate of their existence as well as your own.

As you use Autogenics for one problem, other problems, seemingly unrelated, also disappear because one imbalance produces another.

Arthur, 28, overcame his fear of flying using these methods, and his skin condition cleared.

Jeanne, 41, lost weight using these methods, and her high blood pressure normalized.

Max, 34, improved his jogging endurance and his office relationships improved.

Earlier in this chapter, I listed a number of areas in which Autogenics can be used to alleviate unwanted conditions and situations. The list is just a tiny sample. In truth, the list is endless.

You can have better health.

You can have more money.

You can be loved and respected by more people.

You can get more out of life.

Autogenics is a proven way. It is now up to you to take the next step.

CHAPTER 2

Autogenics for Relief of Common Ailments

IN THIS CHAPTER, we begin the training called Autogenics.

It is a beginning in the sense that we must crawl before we walk, walk before we run.

Yet, even in its simplest form, Autogenics gets us there.

We are going to apply it first to pesky health problems. We are going to see that, by going through the three formulae even in an elementary, beginner's way, dramatic changes can take place. We will see if we can get rid of headache, other chronic pain, insomnia, constipation and similar unwanted physical conditions.

Susan was 19 years old, a junior in college, attractive, and suffering from terrible migraine headaches. When she had an attack, she would have to lie in bed for one, two or three days. She was nauseous and in terrible pain. Her complaint had been diagnosed by several physicians as migraines. She had had them since she was in high school. They occurred generally after a prolonged period of tension. They would start with a mild headache and gradually build. Sometimes the medications that she was given would be effective, most times, not. Her target was to alleviate her migraine headaches.

There had been some biofeedback studies which indicated that concentrating on a sensation of warmth in a hand somehow created a sympathetic response that seemed to relieve migraines. She was asked if her Intelligence Filter could find a pathway to create this warmth in her hand, and by virtue of that, could the migraines then be relieved?

She responded positively. A sequence was planned in which her mind would first react to a diminishment of stress and then to a feeling of warmth in her hand. The change formula worked well. The frequency and severity of the migraine headaches considerably lessened. Soon they were no longer the problem they once were. The last we heard, Susan was a much happier person.

If you have ever had migraine headaches, you know what a blessing Autogenics was for Susan. Considering the small amount of time invested, the absence of drugs with possible side effects, and the resulting effectiveness, Autogenics should be in everybody's "medicine chest."

As originally practiced by Dr. Schultz, Autogenic Training required several practice periods a day, building up to 30-minute sessions and even then the process was in its initial stages.

There were six standard AT exercises which the trainee had to put himself through in sequence. The first required concentration on arms and legs, repeating the phrase, "My arms and legs are heavy." Next came, "My arms and legs are warm." The third exercise brought calm and regular heart function by repeating, "My heart is calm and regular." Four: "My breath is calm and regular." Five: "My solar plexus is warm." And finally, exercise number six: "My forehead is cool."

Perhaps life was at a more leisurely pace in Schultz's day. But today time is money. We look to save time whenever possible. By adapting these lengthy techniques to proven hypnotic procedures, we have succeeded in cutting down the original AT procedures, producing the faster and frequently even more effective Petrie Method® which we term Autogenics.

We still retain the three basic formulae: the mood formula, the relaxation formula, and the change formula. But by utilizing the technique of finger levitation which I will explain in a moment and by enlisting the help of the mind's Intelligence Filter, we cut away huge amounts of time between this moment when you are ready to begin and the moment when you say "Hey!" or "Wow!" or however you express the arrival of that moment of joyful relief.

Experiencing the Mood Formula

Autogenics begins with a mood.

It would not do to begin when you are angry, excited, or disturbed. You cannot attain the relaxation necessary to produce changes in physical or mental behavior.

You can relax deeply if you are in a mood that is conducive to relaxation.

"Wait a minute," you say, "either I am in this kind of a mood or that kind of a mood. I cannot change my mood at will."

I have news for you. You create your own moods. Yes, events in which you are involved affect your moods but they do so only by affecting your decision as to what mood you wish to create.

For instance, you are going on a picnic. The picnic basket is packed with goodies and you are preparing to leave. Just then it starts to pour. As you watch the sky darken and the deluge begin, you decide on a mood—probably one of disappointment or despair. At that same moment, another person who watches the rain begin rejoices. He happens to be a farmer. The rain is money in his pocket. His mood is different from yours.

True, it is not easy to do a mood about-face. As you watch the rain, you cannot change your canceled picnic mood instantly to the farmer's crop improvement mood.

But there are mental procedures to control moods. We are going to use these procedures now to set a typical mood that induces relaxation in body and mind.

First, for contrast, I am going to ask you to use these procedures to set a non-relaxed mood. In a moment I am going to ask you to put the book down and imagine yourself in a certain place. As you imagine yourself there, remember how it feels to be there—remember your mood.

That certain place is crossing the main thoroughfare of your city. Traffic is at its height. You decide to cross against the light. Put the book down, close your eyes, and do it...

How did you feel? Certainly not relaxed. Probably your pulse quickened. You had a sense of danger, excitement, and concern. You probably opened your eyes and ended that frantic scene in a few seconds.

Now try a different place. Again, remember how it feels to be there. This time the place is a peaceful, natural setting, perhaps by a stream or a lake or on a beach. Pick some beautiful, tranquil spot that you can recall. Be there. Enjoy it. Put the book down, close your eyes and do it now...

How did you feel? Certainly it was a different mood from that caused by the traffic scene. You undoubtedly felt a sense of peace. It was more enjoyable. You may have hated to end it, remaining with your eyes closed longer than before.

This is the way you are going to set a relaxed mood for Autogenics. It is enjoying this kind of a mood that is going to be your first step for each application of Autogenics to create a change in your health or happiness and to reinforce that change.

Experiencing the Relaxation Formula

A bird sits on a telephone wire or tree branch. A cat curls up in a chair. A dog lies on the grass, head between his paws. Animals relax naturally. In this busy world, we humans seem to have forgotten how to relax, how to do nothing with our bodies and nothing with our minds.

We are continually active. We are going, going, going. Or we are thinking, thinking, thinking.

Relaxation is revitalization. Our body recuperates from all of the stress of the world while we sleep. We can add to that recuperation by a few minutes a day of awake relaxation, as the animals do.

But because we have forgotten how to do nothing, we need to learn all over again how to be passive physically and mentally. Some people just cannot sit still for any length of time. Most people cannot still their minds for even a minute. Once you acquire a simple procedure for relaxation, you will find that just enjoying a few minutes of this serenity each day can improve your general well-being.

You will feel younger, more energetic, more in control of your life.

But there is much more to relaxation than that. While you are relaxed, statements you make to yourself and pictures you hold in your mind concerning yourself, are able to reach the deep brain centers where they are accepted and stored. This constitutes programming. You literally can program yourself, while relaxed, to be healthier, act differently, perform more skillfully.

So relaxation is a valuable state to reach. It pays to be able to relax. It is well worth the few minutes of methodology that you must go through. After awhile, these step-by-step procedures become more natural to you and you can sit down and go through them almost automatically.

But first you need to read these steps over two or three times, then put the book down, close your eyes and experience them as best you remember them. Later, you will have someone read to you, or you will make a tape and listen to your own voice instructing you.

What will you be telling yourself? Here is a sample. Just read this for interest now and don't worry about remembering it:

> Make yourself comfortable and close your eyes. Allow yourself to become limp. Allow all the muscles in your body to become slack. Notice your breathing. Notice the movement as you breathe in and out. As you breathe in, notice the filling of air in your lungs, and the upward movement of your chest. Notice the opposite movement as you breathe out. Breathe a little deeper now. Feel the difference. Breathe slowly and rhythmically in a normal way.
>
> Each time you breathe out, feel yourself sinking lower into a relaxed calmness. As you continue to breathe rhythmically in this fashion, deliberately allow yourself to sink down deeper each time you exhale. Each time you exhale, you associate the air leaving your lungs with the sensation of pleasantly sinking deeper and deeper.
>
> As you do this, you begin to become sensitive to the tensions in your muscles. Breathe in and as you exhale, release these tensions. Focus your mind on one area of your body. Start from the toes to your ankles. Breathe in and as you allow the air to smoothly escape, release the muscles and the tensions from your toes, ankles and feet. Do it again. Release all of the stress, all strain from the area of your toes to your ankles.

Now permit your mind to encompass a greater area from your toes to your thighs. Visualize the area from your toes to your thighs and this time as you inhale, get ready so that when you exhale you can allow every muscle, every fiber, every nerve to relax from your toes all the way up to your thighs.

Now breathe in. Exhale. Let the relaxation take place. Again, breathe in. Again exhale and feel the relaxation take place. Now visualize the area from your toes all the way up into your chest. Include the muscles in your back. Visualize that whole area from your toes all the way to your chest, front and back. Now, again, breathe in and exhale; feel the relaxation from your toes to your chest, including all the muscles in your back. Once again, inhale, exhale, relax.

Finally, visualize your whole body from your toes to your thighs to your chest, throughout your back, including your shoulders, your neck, your head, your face and even the muscles in your jaw. Visualize your whole body. Now inhale. Slowly exhale. Feel your whole body sinking down, down, down in comfort, relaxation and limpness. Do it again. Inhale and exhale, sinking down deeper.

You have now reached a blissful degree of relaxation but you can reach even deeper and more healthful stages. Imagine a flight of stairs. Think of them as being wide and very safe. There are 10 stairs and you are standing on the top step. Now, one step at a time, you are going to slowly and safely descend the stairs. And with each step, you'll descend into a deeper and deeper state of profound relaxation. Wait until you exhale. Now slowly descend the first step and relax, peacefully, comfortable, restful. Now, as you exhale descend the second step. Relax, down, peaceful. Your body and your mind are calm, comfortable. Now, as you exhale, descend the third step, slowly floating down, down. As you exhale, go down the fourth step. Now take a nice deep breath and as you exhale, go down the fifth step. And now another breath and as you exhale, go down the sixth step. Another breath and as you exhale, go down the seventh step. And another breath, down the eighth step. And another breath, down the ninth. Another breath, all the way down to the tenth step.

Now just float. Float as if you were in a big billowy cloud, soft and comfortable. Just float. Do nothing. Just completely relax, deeper and deeper.

In a few moments, you will count to 10. When you reach 10, you will open your eyes, you will feel wide awake. You will feel completely relaxed and mentally and physically calmed and

> composed. You will feel at a high level of well-being, better than you felt before. As your count moves closer to 10, the feeling of heaviness, of limpness, of lethargy will completely disappear. With each number you become more and more wide awake, feeling composed and restored: Now, 1, 2, 3, 4, 5, 6, 7, 8, 9, 10. Wide awake! Wide awake!

Now read it over again. This time, note the major steps. There are really only four major steps. See if you can identify these four basic steps as you read the above passage for the second time. Do it now...

The four major steps can be summed up as follows:

1. Sit comfortably, close your eyes and relax.
2. Be aware of your breathing, relaxing more and more of your body with each exhalation, starting with the toes.
3. Imagine a flight of ten stairs and step slowly down each, exhaling and relaxing more with each step down.
4. Count from one to ten, first reminding yourself that when you reach ten, you will be wide awake, feeling great.

Looking at these four major steps, you can see that the long passage indented above is really not hard to remember. The words are less important than the action.

To experience this relaxation now, all you need to do is read these four steps again, put the book down and do it. I'll wait. Do it now...

You have just experienced the second formula. It should have been a pleasant, comfortable event. You are probably rested and rejuvenated. You might even feel "rarin to go." Certainly, every cell of your body has benefited by this relief from stress.

There is nothing weird or strange about the feeling of relaxation. It is a natural state. It does not really have to be "learned." When you turn off the outside world by crawling into your bed at night, you are turning on this relaxed state. The difference is that you do not remain awake to use it for benefits. You are not in control of it when you doze off.

By remaining awake in this relaxed state, you remain in control of it—able to use it to give your mind instructions for helping yourself in whatever way you wish.

Before we go on to experience the third and last Autogenics formula—the change formula—I want to give you a word of advice about your attitude at this point.

Many people who go through a relaxation procedure for the first time are concerned about whether they are really relaxing deeply enough. You may be wondering whether you relaxed really deeply when you just went through the four steps. Hear is a simple way to insure your relaxation:

Stop worrying about it. Be relaxed about relaxing.

If you are "up tight" about relaxing or anxious about how well you are relaxing, you are interfering with your own relaxation. You are getting in your own way.

Accept however deeply you are relaxing. Even if you are relaxing only superficially, you will get better each time you do it, because it becomes more familiar to you. The only pitfall is anxiety about it. Resolve now that you are on your way. Know it.

Be relaxed about relaxing.

Experiencing the Change Formula

Tonight tens of millions of Americans will toss and turn in bed worrying whether they will be able to get to sleep before dawn. They are the victims of insomnia. It afflicts over 25 million Americans all of the time and millions of others occasionally.

About a quarter-billion dollars a year is spent on prescription sleeping pills alone in an attempt to conquer this problem. Yet these pills can ruin both the days and the nights of insomniacs.

In a 1976 report by doctors at Stanford University's Sleep Disorder Clinic, it was pointed out that 40 percent of patients who complain of insomnia are actually losing sleep because they have become dependent on the very pills they were taking to get rid of their insomnia. When they are gradually taken off these pills, they sleep on the average of 20 percent more, with many claiming they are free of sleep problems altogether.

One man, who was taking six different sleeping potions—a

total of 8,000 milligrams of drugs a night for 30 years—and getting nowhere with the problem, when gradually withdrawn from this medication, increased his sleeping time from 4½ to 6½ hours per night.

My purpose in discussing insomnia with you is, whether it is a problem for you or not, that you will enjoy a better night's sleep tonight.

Why will you sleep better? Because you are going to experience the third formula of Autogenics, the change formula, to go from awake to asleep.

If you are an insomniac, the dividends of this change will be immense for you. If you are accustomed to falling asleep readily, you will still see the formula at work and, in the process, learn Autogenics for other areas where a need exists for you. Before this chapter is finished, I will show you how to alter the change formula to get rid of other pesky health problems, such as relieving cold symptoms, headaches, constipation, nausea, pain, and allergies.

Mary, a single woman, was on heavy medication for her insomnia. The pills worked for her during the night. They also worked during the day. She felt dopey until mid-afternoon and found it difficult to function in her job. Mary used the change formula you are about to experience. She used it successfully both to fall asleep and to reduce the number of pills she was taking. She was soon off the pills, sleeping better, and feeling alive all day.

The change formula is inserted into your routine just before ending your relaxation. It is simple. You tell yourself how to change. Of course, tonight, experiencing the change formula for falling asleep, you will not end your relaxation. You will go to sleep from the relaxed state.

Because you are relaxed, telling yourself how to change, seeing yourself change, feeling the way you want to feel actually produces new programming to behave you in that way.

You are going to understand that better when you use it tonight to fall asleep.

Tomorrow morning you will be able to read on, learning how to use the mood formula, the relaxation formula, and the change formula to improve yourself in other ways. We will also learn how to apply these formulae more effectively, using techniques derived not only from Dr. Schultz's work with Autogenic Training but my years of experience with tens of thousands of people with every kind of problem you can think of.

The change formula for falling asleep takes place when you have reached a deep state of relaxation using the relaxation formula. You then count backwards starting at 500. Between each descending number, you tell yourself you are getting drowsier and drowsier, sleepier and sleepier.

It does not matter what words you use. Here are mine, but do not memorize them—use your own words:

> 500. With each lower number I get more and more drowsy. 499. Sleepier and sleepier. 498. Nothing disturbs me. 497. Deeper and deeper toward sleep. 496. Drifting closer to sleep. 495. Drowsier and drowsier. 494. Deeper and deeper. 493. Drifting deeper and deeper. 492. Getting sleepier and sleepier. 491. Sleepier and sleepier. 490. Deeper and deeper. 489. Sleepier. 488. Deeper. 487...

The countdown procedure is irresistible. It blocks out the thoughts that keep us awake. Few people ever have to go below 400. You may not get down as far as 450. Even if you do have to continue to count longer, don't be concerned because any moment... you...will...be...

I suggest that you put the book down now beside your bed and discontinue further reading until you are ready to retire. I will then give you details of how to proceed.

It is now bedtime. You are undressed and preparing for a good night's sleep. Here are the steps to take once you turn off the light and crawl beneath the covers.

1. Create a sleeping mood by closing your eyes and imagining a sleeping place. Nothing is happening. Everybody is taking a siesta. You feel sleepy.
2. Be aware of your breathing, as you did in the relaxation formula, relaxing more and more of your body from toes to head on each exhalation.
3. Walk down those ten imaginary stairs, feeling more and more limp and relaxed with each step.
4. Begin your countdown from 500, telling yourself how each count makes you sleepier and sleepier.

The next thing you know it will be morning. Have a good night's sleep...

How These Three Formulae Equal Better Health for You

Each of these formulae—the mood, relaxation, and change—is a hypnotic technique.

Can hypnotic techniques affect the workings of the body? To answer that question, let me take you through a few minutes' experience in my office in Great Neck, Long Island, that has happened again and again.

The telephone rings. It is the local hospital. A patient in surgery is hemorrhaging. Can I come immediately? Yes. In a few minutes, I am in the operating room. I ask the surgeon for the patient's name. It is Jennifer. She is under the effects of a general anesthesia. I see the blood flowing from the opening in her abdomen.

"Jennifer," I say in a commanding voice. "You are aware of my voice. You are to do what I say. You are to stop bleeding now." Several times I repeat, "Stop bleeding now." As I watch, the bleeding slowly trickles to a halt. I leave.

This is an extreme case of the mind accepting instructions and changing the way it is performing the body.

At the other extreme is the next example. You are relaxed watching a soap opera on television. A commercial comes on. It tells you that Brand X white bread is nutritious. It shows happy, healthy people eating Brand X bread. The commercial ends and the soap opera returns. You forget all about Brand X bread. Right?

Wrong.

You were in a tranquil mood. You were relaxed. When the X-Brand commercial asked you to switch to its bread, this was a change formula. Whether you realized it or not, that commercial had reprogrammed your behavior. The next time in a supermarket you would automatically reach out for X-Brand bread.

We get sick for the same reason. We accept programming to get sick. Sometimes others give us that programming unintentionally by telling us about their sciatica, their bursitis, or their arthritis. Sometimes we give it to ourself by saying such things as:

"He gives me a pain in the neck."
"She makes me sick."
"Oh, my aching back."
"I can't stand it."
"He galls me."

We have scores of programming statements that dot our daily conversation. When they are repeated enough, you do not need to be relaxed for such a change formula to be effective.

It is said we are born with about two thousand perfect programmings for the running of our body. Then the you-know-what hits the fan. We pollute these perfect health programmings with anxiety, tension, worry, fear, hostility, anger, rivalry, and a score or more of stressful attitudes and reactions.

We create too much uric acid and get gout. We impede our elimination system and get toxic. We tighten up with tension and create a multiplicity of imbalances in our once perfect programming and, as a result, we find we have high blood pressure, intestinal problems, or arteriosclerosis.

The mind makes us sick. We are responsible. It is our mind, our thoughts, our stress. But I have good news for you.

The mind can also make us well.

You now know the basic procedure by which you change what you want in your life. You can apply these procedures to health matters and they work. The mind runs the body.

You can apply these procedures to skills, abilities, personality, and happiness because the mind is also in charge of these.

You can even apply these principles to relationships with other people where apparently your mind is not the only mind in charge. And yet your Intelligence Filter knows the way out of such human mazes and it works here, too.

We start with health because nothing else can take priority over that. We cannot apply our skills or enjoy rewarding human relations if health is a problem.

We have started with insomnia as the first of the health problems. Insomnia is most easily understood and accepted by you as "mental." This is one reason why we began with it, but there is another. Insomnia can be the cause of other physical ailments.

Gladys, a middle-aged woman married to a physician, had a whole bunch of physical problems. She had pains in her legs, pains in hands, and pains in her feet. Her abdomen gave her distress. She had frequent headaches. She complained of double vision, and insomnia. When she brought these to her doctor-husband, he became impatient with her, claiming that she was a hypochondriac just bidding for his attention.

When she came to us, she asked only for help with the insomnia. But since she had told us the whole story, we recognized the connection between these ailments, the insomnia, and the cause of the insomnia: her less-than-perfect marital situation.

Gladys went through the three Autogenics formulae to fall asleep—setting the tranquil mood, relaxing, and the countdown. When it worked, she not only was sleeping better but the pains began to recede. She felt better in every way. She then agreed to add a few more change formulae and go through the Autogenics procedure to correct the basic situation.

Before ending her relaxation, she gave herself the following instructions for change:

> *"I will be more and more independent, able to stand up on my own two feet."*
>
> *"Every day I will physically be stronger and fitter, emotionally stronger and fitter."*

One by one all of Gladys' ailments disappeared. Her marital relations improved. Her quality of life rose immeasurably.

Using the Formulae for Specific Health Problems

If you have used the three formulae to fall asleep, whether or not you suffer from insomnia, you have practiced them, experienced them, made them more familiar to you.

You are now ready to use them on a wide variety of physical ailments. We are going to divide these ailments into two groups: common ailments and serious health problems.

We will start with the common ailments in this chapter because they respond at least to a degree to your use of the three formulae in their simplest form as you have already experienced.

In the next chapter, you will improve your use of the three formulae so that they can be effective against more serious health problems.

This does not mean that you cannot wait and use the advanced techniques of Chapter 3 for common ailments. In fact, I recommend that you do go through the procedures of Chapter 3 if you want more sure-fire results with common ailments. But for those of you who are impatient and want at least some benefits now, here is how to use what you already know for:

Allergy	Constipation	Complexion
Pain	Contact Lens Difficulty	Backache
Headache	Nausea	Cold Symptoms

Let's go over the change formulae for each in turn.

Allergy. Allergies can manifest as respiratory problems, skin problems and other physical problems. Specialists have identified hundreds of substances to which people can become allergic, ranging from the more common pollens to the less common cat's fur, bird feathers, and synthetic fibers.

Whatever the cause of your allergy, identified or not, it will have less and less effect on you as you use Autogenics. The change formula is directed at the effect, not the cause. If you know the cause, you can reinforce the results with a change formula worded to include the cause; however, this is not essential.

Here is the change formula for an allergy. Describe the symptom it manifests for you.

"My eyes are comfortable. My eye muscles are relaxed and at ease under all normal conditions. There is no smarting or excessive tearing."

Or,

"My nose is clear. My breathing is easy. There is no congestion, running, or stuffiness."

Or,

"My skin is perfect. It is uniform in color and texture."

If you know the cause, word the change order in this way:

"Dogs' hair is harmless to me. My nose is not affected by it. I breathe easily without difficulty of any type whether exposed to dogs' hair or not."

Word your change formula simply and directly. Then set the mood, relax, use the change formula by making the statement silently to yourself, then end by counting yourself up feeling wide awake.

Constipation. If you are eating properly, your bowels should be moving properly. If they do not, there could be some mental programming that needs to be counteracted. First, check your diet. It should include roughage like raw fruit, raw vegetables, whole grains, especially bran.

Second, you do not need to know the mental cause but it helps if you do. Is there any expression you use that could bear on the problem (i.e., "tough shit.")? Is there any problem having to do with your inability to get around that you worry about? Do you consider yourself "tight" financially? These are the kinds of attitudes that frequently affect bowel movement.

Here is the change formula for constipation, first without a known cause, then with.

"My bowels move easily and on schedule."
"My bowels move easily and on schedule. No events or circumstances bother me, such as (insert suspected cause) so as to interfere with normal evacuation."

Complexion. Dermatologists now largely agree that most skin problems are triggered by stress. Your use of the relaxation formula in Autogenics is the beginning of relief from complexion problems. The change formula to further that relief is:

"I do not need these blemishes. My skin is becoming more and more attractive each day."

Or,

"These warts will fall off...
These blackheads will stop forming...
These pimples will disappear...
My skin is becoming clear and attractive."

Pain. Pain is subjective. It is not measurable by any equipment. The doctor must ask you about the pain. If you have chronic pain, it is quite possible that you are programmed to have it. It started; it continued; you expected it; you got in the habit of having it.

So frequently the body has already corrected the original cause of the pain, yet we still expect it and so we still experience it. This kind of pain responds quickly to Autogenics. If your pain does not respond to the method provided now, use the more advanced method provided in Chapter 3.

We are going to turn subjective pain into something objective. It will therefore no longer be pain. Here is how the change formula for pain is as follows:

Give it a location (point to it). Give it a shape. (What kind of container would fit it best?) Give it a color. (If it had a color, what color would it be?) Give it an appropriate taste. Give it an appropriate smell. Repeat again if some pain remains, noting changes in location, shape, color, taste, and smell. Repeat a third time, if necessary.

Remember, always use your mood and relaxation formulae before using the change formula. Also remember to end by counting yourself up to a state of "wide awake, feeling great."

Even people with several years of bursitis or pinched nerve pains have experienced total and permanent relief with this simple procedure. The pain habit is broken. If your pain does not respond, wait until Chapter 3.

Headache. Headaches come and go. They could be simple tension headaches or more serious migraine headaches.

First use the objective technique. If the headache is still there, go through the mood and relaxation formulae and use this change formula.

> *"I do not need this headache. When I count to ten and open my eyes, the headache will be gone."*

If there is still some remnant of headache left, wait a few minutes and repeat.

If you know the cause, such as time pressure, word your change formula to fit the cause. For example:

"I have all the time I need. Everything is working out in good time. I am comfortable with my rate of progress."

Stubborn migraine headaches might have to wait for the more powerful change formula for pain given in the next chapter.

Backache. Use the objective change formula. If not totally effective, repeat your Autogenics session using this change formula.

"My back is perfect. All bones and joints move in harmony."

Should you suspect the mental cause, you can help prevent future backaches by directing your change formula at this cause. Such as:

"Responsibility is weightless. I handle it effortlessly. I am capable and confident."

Cold Symptoms. Colds are "caught" when resistance to germs or viruses goes down. You can lower your resistance in many ways—mostly all related to stress. You also have been programmed to catch a cold when certain events take place—getting your feet wet, sitting in a draft, be in the same room with somebody with a cold.

A hypnotized subject is told that a red-hot poker will touch his hand, then he is touched with a cool spoon. A blister forms.

The body strictly obeys programming. It will just as strictly obey your Autogenics programming. Here is the change formula for a cold.

"My throat feels better and better. My breathing becomes easier and easier."

And to include possible causes in the cold change formula:

"My resistance is high. I am not affected by negative suggestions, such as warnings about colds. I am resourceful and capable. Problems are challenges. I do not succumb to them; I overcome them."

Nausea. Most gastro-intestinal problems are caused by worry and tension. The discovery that the stomach becomes inflamed when the emotions become disturbed was a breakthrough to our present understanding of the mind-body relationship. Here are both the basic and the cause-related change formulae for nausea and chronic stomach distress.

> *"My stomach problem lessens in frequency and intensity. My stomach is restored to a healthy state and operates normally."*

To help prevent the further causation of the problem, also this:

> *"I become more calm and relaxed in everyday matters. I am free of worry. I do not get easily excited. I am serene and confident."*

Contact Lens Difficulty. As contact lenses become more popular, the need to get accustomed to them is becoming a more prevalent problem. Here is the needed change formula to make their application and wearing easier for you.

> *"I put on my contact lenses quickly and easily, I am not tense. My eyes surrender to them. They become more and more natural to me the longer I wear them."*

Repeating the procedures for all of these change formulae:

Step 1. Induce a tranquil mood with the mood formula.
Step 2. Induce relaxation with the relaxation formula.
Step 3. Induce a change with the change formula.

In the next chapter, you will learn how to improve the initial formulae, which you experienced in this chapter, for more dramatic applications and success.

CHAPTER 3

Autogenics for Serious Health Problems

IN THIS CHAPTER, we increase the effectiveness of the three formulae of Autogenics so that we can use them for more serious health problems.

We will use these strengthened formulae also for the other changes in our life that the next chapters will confront—changes for the better in our social life, business life and family life.

As we strengthen these formulae, we reach deeper into the recesses of the brain for stronger programming. Here are the neurons that affect every cell of our body.

Most of us are vaguely aware that our body is composed of small units called cells. But we do not realize how these cells are constantly growing, multiplying, and dying. In effect, we have an almost new body every few months.

These tiny elaborate organisms called cells form all of our bodies' bones, muscles, organs and tissues. These appear to be quite solid in nature. Yet, the cells themselves are composed of atoms. Atoms are infinitesimally small but are quite spacious. That is, the size of the atom's nucleus or center compared to the electrons that rotate around it is comparable to the size of our sun compared to the planets that rotate around it, with spaces between also in proportion. So you might say that an atom is as spacious as space itself.

This concept helps us to understand how tiny electrical messages sent by our brain neurons as a result of our thoughts can effect solid matter, like our backs, our stomachs, our kidneys.

Tiny electrical impulses that you can create by using your mood formula ready the cells of your body for relaxation and change. Tiny electrical impulses you create by using your relaxation formula quiet the cells of your body by relieving them of stress and permitting them to grow and function normally. Tiny electrical impulses that you create by using your change formula cause the target cells for which they are intended to normalize and revitalize.

Direct these thoughts at whatever part of your body is in need of normalizing and you succeed in making very real, noticeable changes for the better.

Hypnotic techniques are being used more and more by health professionals to assist in all types of therapy. And hypnotic techniques are being taught more and more to the average person as a tool for self-help.

The high cost of medical care is driving more and more people to take better care of themselves and to become more responsible for their own good health. Autogenics is a valuable means for maintaining high levels of abounding good health. It is not meant to take the place of medical care but it can help you to help your doctor.

Autogenics is both a preventive tool and a corrective tool. It lowers your medical costs by enabling you to maintain good health and to restore good health should you fall prey to some health problem. It also serves to make you more comfortable during the period of recuperation from illness.

It is to this factor—the relief of pain—that we will direct our attention first, providing stronger formulae for stubborn pains or more intense pains than those we addressed in the previous chapter.

How to Strengthen the Mood Formula

We can all alleviate pain.

Have you ever seen a child fall and the parents begin to laugh? Seldom does such a child cry. The child is more likely to cry if the parents do not notice the fall or if the parents act quite frightened and concerned about the fall.

Is the child's pain any less because of a certain type of parental reaction. Yes, it is. You are making your pain more intense or less intense by your own reactions to it.

The person who tenses up in a dentist's chair even before the "open wide" is presenting himself or herself as a candidate for pain. It will certainly be more pain than that experienced by the person who relaxes and even thinks about something else.

The mind, busy thinking of something else, cuts off pain. You cannot think of two things at the same time. When you are finished thinking, you suddenly "remember" that you have a headache or some other pain.

These are not the only ways that the mind can effect pain, as you probably may have experienced in Chapter 2. The mind can actually numb pain.

A special change formula in which we create a numbness in our hand and then transfer that numbness to a pain somewhere in our body will be discussed shortly. A mood formula that sets the stage for that particular change formula will be more effective than a mood formula that merely sets the stage for relaxation.

Since the change formula requires you to hold your hand in an imaginary bucket of ice water, any mood formula involving the feeling of cold will prepare the way effectively.

Some suggestions might be:

- Imagine yourself at a picnic, reaching into the ice bucket to serve cold soda or beer to everybody.
- Imagine yourself making a snow man without gloves.
- Picture a winter scene through frosty window panes that you attempt to clear with your bare hands.

You should spend at least a minute or two "living" the scene you create. I have not painted much detail into the above three examples. I will leave the details to you, to be supplied by your own past experiences. It is preferable to choose a scene that you can remember having experienced rather than one you have read about or have heard somebody else describe.

When you draw on your own memory, you trigger brain neurons to respond again as they did then and this means the desired numbness will result.

Let's say you remember wading into frigid water one winter. Use your few minutes of mood formula application to remember it in detail. For example:

> You are standing at the edge of a mountain lake. It is surrounded by tall stately trees. There are snow-capped mountains in the distant. The air is crisp and cold. The sky is blue. The water is quiet and inviting. You wonder how cold it is. You take off your shoes and socks to test it. Right, it is icy cold. But you enjoy the fresh feeling. You wade out. Your feet hurt at first from the cold, but then they grow numb. Your feet become so numb that they feel like sticks. The sun warms the rest of your body. You plunge your hands into the water to feel its iciness as you turn and wade back to the shore.

You do not need someone to read this to your; nor do you need to make a tape of it to play back to yourself. Your mind will fill in the details as you relive a frigid experience.

Any frigid experience will set the mood for the pain-relief change formula.

Any experience will set the mood for other change formulae if selected with that change formula in mind. More examples of this later. We will also provide ways to improve the relaxation mood formula which has general application.

Deepening the Relaxation

The best way to get better results in Autogenics is to relax more deeply. Enhancement of your relaxation formula should now receive your top priority.

The best way to relax more deeply is to have somebody read relaxation instructions to you. Or, you can give these instructions to yourself by making a cassette tape. After you finish your mood formula, you turn on the tape and relax.

The following relaxation discourse takes about 10 to 15 minutes. If it is being read to you by another person, or by yourself into a cassette tape, here are the rules to follow:

- Read at a slow, consistent rate.
- Do not read with emotion or feeling; the voice should be more monotone.
- The vocal approach should be mildly authoritarian—these are orders to be followed.

This relaxation formula has been changed from the one in the previous chapter to better fit the change formula. Because the change formula involves the use of the hand—making it numb in imaginary ice cold water so the numbness can be passed on to a pained area—so this relaxation formula involves the use of the hand.

You will create a warmth and heaviness in your left hand (right hand if you are left-handed). You will cause a finger to rise. You will cause your hand and arm to rise from your lap. When you are ready, you will permit it to drop back on your lap. There will be more instructions for heaviness and limpness.

The change formula for pain relief will follow immediately. And the discourse will end with the one to ten count to bring you up to full wakefulness, feeling better than before.

A combination of finger levitation and hand levitation, this is an effective relaxation formula. You may use it for other Autogenics purposes, in which case you would flip the tape off where the pain change formula begins and provide your own one to ten count to end the session.

When using this relaxation for pain relief, you do not have to be in pain at the time you use it. You can go through the three formulae while feeling fine and you will be pre-programming yourself for relieving pain at some future time. Later, when pain strikes, you can go through an abbreviated mood, relaxation, and change formula from memory, create a numbed hand in seconds and transfer that numbness.

Here is the strengthened relaxant formula.

A Relaxation Formula for Relieving Pain

I want you to sit comfortably in your chair and relax, keeping your eyes open. As you sit there, place both hands palms down on your thighs. Look at your left hand and look at it very carefully. Be aware of its feeling. Be as sensitive as you can to whatever feelings, whatever sensations that you notice in your hand. Keep your eyes on your hand and as you relax your hand, you will notice certain things happen. Concentrate on all the sensations, all the feelings. Be aware of whatever feelings you feel in your hand, no matter what they are. Perhaps you may feel the heaviness of your hand as it lies perfectly relaxed on your thigh. Perhaps you can feel the warmth of your hand as it rests there. No matter what sensations there are, I want you to observe them. Keep watching your hand, notice how still it is, how it remains in one position. There is actually some movement there. Subtle movement at first. And this movement will soon become noticeable, although it may not be noticeable yet. I want you to keep watching your hand. Even if your attention wanders from your hand, it will always return. So keep watching it, and wondering when the motion will show itself. Expect the motion to show itself soon. Now focus your mind on the finger next to your thumb of your left hand. Look at that finger. Soon, that finger is going to move. Keep watching it. You will begin to notice a slight movement. As the movement begins, you will notice that very slowly the finger will begin to lift. It will begin to lift up slowly. The space between your finger and your thigh will slowly widen. As soon as you see the finger moving, as soon as you see it making even the tiniest upward movement, I want you to voluntarily close your eyes. So as soon as you see it lifting, as soon as you see the smallest motion, I want you to voluntarily close your eyes. Now your finger is becoming lighter. Lighter and lighter. You are becoming aware of the feeling of lightness in your finger. It feels like a feather. It feels as if a balloon is lifting it up and up into the air. Lifting, lifting the finger up and up and up. Pulling it up higher and higher. As your finger lifts, you will feel the feelings of lifting spreading into all of your left hand, into all the fingers of your left hand. Now all of your hand is becoming lighter. It will slowly lift and rise as if it were being lifted up and up. You feel more relaxed with your eyes closed. It is being pulled up higher. Higher and higher, the entire hand becoming very light. Lighter and lighter. As this feeling of lightness continues, you become more and more relaxed. As you become relaxed, the feeling of lightness drifts all through your hand into all the fingers and the palm of your hand. It spreads into your wrist and into your arm. So now your arm can begin to feel the lightness and your arm can begin to feel lighter and lighter and lighter. It can slowly lift and rise like a feather. It is as if a balloon were lifting it up into the air lifting it up and up and up. Pulling it higher and higher and higher. The arm is becoming very light. As you keep feeling the lightness in your hand and in your arm, so you are becoming more and more deeply relaxed. And as it continues to rise, you will slowly but steadily go into a deeper and deeper state of relaxation, your hand is becoming lighter, your arm lighter, lighter. You are becoming so deeply relaxed now. So deeply relaxed. In a few moments, I'm going to stop talking and your arm can rise as high as it needs to. As it rises, you go deeper and deeper. (Pause about ten seconds.)

Just allow your arm to rise as high as it needs to. And when it has reached the point that satisfies you, allow it to drop limply down, down to your thigh and enjoy the wonderful, pleasant sensation of your deep relaxation. Perhaps you want to let it drop now. Just sit back comfortably with your eyes closed and let yourself go as limp as you can. Make yourself go limp—slack. Let all the muscles of your body relax. And as you let the muscles relax, feel them relaxing. Be aware that they are relaxing. Relax them so completely that you actually feel them relaxed. Don't hold yourself together. Go limp and slack. Let the muscles of your feet, of your ankles relax. Let the muscles of your legs relax. Let them go limp and slack. And once you do this, you might begin to feel that you can sense the relaxation. The limper you allow your feet to go, the heavier they become. Eventually they will feel as heavy as lead. And the same way, the muscles in your shoulders and your back, let them go completely. Let the muscles in your arms and your back relax. Let them go limp and slack. And as you continue with these feelings of relaxation, you will begin to feel heavier and heavier, as if you're beginning to sink down and down. If you find that you are tensing in any way, either mentally or physically, just be aware of it and let yourself go. Give yourself up completely to this pleasant sensation of relaxing. Enjoy this relaxed, drowsy, comfortable feeling. As you do so, you will begin to feel the sensations of heaviness spreading all through your body as if your whole body is becoming as heavy as lead. As if it wanted to sink down and down, deeper and deeper. Allow yourself to sink back comfortably, deeper and deeper. It is a comfortably pleasant sensation. As you feel it, you will become aware of another sensation. It is the sensation of peacefulness, relaxed without concerns, without anxieties and you will feel comfortable. It is one of the most comfortable feelings you have ever experienced. You are gradually now becoming more and more completely at ease. You are able to relax and listen quietly to my voice. You listen to what I am saying. I want you to do nothing else but be aware of my voice. As you listen, as you are aware of my voice, you will feel your body relaxing and you will relax more and more. And all the suggestions that I will give you will have the effect that we want them to have.

A Powerful Change Formula for Relieving Pain

For every day now you will become physically stronger and fitter. You will become more alert, more wide awake, more energetic. You will become much less easily tired, much less easily fatigued, much less easily discouraged. You are relaxing more deeply now. This delightful relaxation is spreading through your legs, into your arms, into your hands, all through your body. Soon you will have another sensation. You will feel as if you were drifting closer and closer towards the feeling of sleep. A kind of a drowsy feeling. As you continue listening to my voice, you feel this drowsiness, a kind of heaviness spreading over you, as if your body were getting very, very heavy. And all of the areas of your body are becoming heavier, and the combination of the heaviness. And the drifting towards drowsiness. Your right hand is very heavy and warm. There is a bucket of ice water by the right side of your chair. Drop your right hand down the side of your chair into this bucket of ice water.

Feel the icy coldness. Feel the ice cubes. Your hand is getting colder and colder. It is getting numb with cold. More numb with every passing second. Keep your hand in the bucket of ice water until I tell you to take it out. When I tell you to take it out, you will test it for numbness by pinching it with your other hand. The cold, icy water does not bother you now, because your hand has become so numb. It continues to grow more and more numb as I talk to you. After you take your hand out of the water when I tell you to do so, and after you have tested it for numbness, I will ask you to touch the part of your body that is in pain and you will be able to pass the numbness on to that part of your body, causing the pain to diminish and disappear. Continue to keep your hand in the icy water, permitting it to get more and more numb. After you have transferred this numbness to relieve pain, you will restore your hand to normal by saying my hand is normal. Now prepare to take your hand out of the bucket of ice water. Place it on your lap. Using your other hand, test the cold hand for numbness. Now touch any pained area with this hand, transferring the numbness. If you cannot reach the pained area with that hand, first transfer the numbness to your other hand by placing the numb hand over it for a second. When you have transferred the numbness from your hand to the pained area, instruct all feeling to return to your numb hand. Just say "My hand is now normal." and your hand is now as it was before you placed it in the cold water. You will now end your relaxation at the count of ten. One, beginning to feel more wide awake. Two, three, four, five. Feeling more awake with each count. Six, seven, eight. Opening your eyes at the count of ten, feeling wonderful. Nine, ten! Eyes open! Feeling great!

More About Pain

Pain is nature's way of signaling trouble. We should respect pain by seeking medical advice if it persists. Under no conditions, use this Autogenics way of deadening pain repeatedly as a continuing method of relief.

Use it in an emergency or when temporary relief is needed until you can see a doctor. Consider it as "first aid." If pain persists, let your doctor interpret nature's message and help you with corrective action.

Pain that persists despite medical attention is a candidate for Autogenics relief steps. Who needs chronic pain? Its message has been received. It is now appropriate to turn it off.

The blessing of the Autogenics way of pain relief is that, once you use it, you do not have to go through a long procedure to use it again. Merely by your remembering that you can make your hand numb, it becomes numb, and you are able to touch the pained area and the pain is gone.

All pain and illness start with a cause. The cause of a pain may not be a twisted ankle or strained muscles. It could be a twisted emotion or strained feelings. The cause of an illness may not be a germ or a virus. It could be a conflict or fear that lowered your resistance.

Part of the Autogenics approach to pain relief and illness control is identifying the cause and programming for a correction of that cause. Treating a symptom can lead to relief of that symptom but the relief might be temporary if the cause is not recognized and "handled."

Before this chapter is over, I am going to give you a change formula for relieving symptoms of each of several illnesses. But I would be remiss were I to ignore causes and just help you treat the symptoms. Causes respond to Autogenics just as successfully as do pain and other distressing symptoms.

The approach is unique. It entails the use of a pendulum. You can create a pendulum by attaching a button to a 12-inch piece of string. The bigger the button and the finer the string, the better. A metal washer is also good.

The purpose of the pendulum is to establish an easy way for your Intelligence Filter to provide you with answers to key questions.

Using the Pendulum to Identify Causes of Pains and Ailments

The way the pendulum provides a line of communication with the deep recesses of the mind is through the tiny musculature of the arm, hand, and fingers, Once you establish this line of communication with the pendulum, you can ask your mind a question and observe the movement of the pendulum. This movement, by previous agreement with our mind, indicates "yes" or "no." By a series of logically sequential questions, you can arrive at the person, event, time, and place of the cause of a physical or mental problem.

Bob, 36, was plagued with upset stomachs. Nausea and vomiting, normally associated with food poisoning, occurred after the simplest of meals. Medications did not help. The doctor wanted him to go to the hospital for a number of expensive and possibly risky tests. Suspecting there was an emotional cause, he came to me. In a few minutes, he was able to use the pendulum—as you will be. He asked if the stomach problem was due to food. The answer was no. Did it have to do with his business? No. His father-in-law was putting pressure on him to leave that business and go into his stockbrokerage firm; did it have something to do with that? Yes.

So in a few minutes, Bob had identified the cause of his continuing problem. This cause was addressed in subsequent Autogenics sessions. He built up his confidence and independence and the trouble was gone.

How does a button on a string answer "yes" or "no"?

It just takes two single steps for you to establish this communication. It is time worth spent. The dividends can be priceless to you.

Be seated on a chair next to a table. Hold the pendulum by the string, placing your elbow on the table so the button or washer can swing freely. Your wrist is bent. Your arm is in a comfortable position. You are ready to go through two steps to establish communications through the pendulum.

Step One. Steady the pendulum. Close your eyes. Visualize the pendulum moving from side to side, left to right, right to left. Imagine that it is swinging from side to side. "See" it swinging. Make the picture vivid, real. Now open your eyes and see if there is indeed a slight side-to-side movement. If not, continue to imagine it swinging side to side until it actually begins to swing this way. When it does, go through the same procedure with a to-and-fro motion, toward you and away from you. Next, try for a clockwise motion. Finally, cause a counter-clockwise motion. Keep practicing until you get a pronounced swing each time before going on to Step Two.

Step Two. What you did in Step One you can now forget. You will never have to control the pendulum again by visualizing. It is moved by your subconscious mind from now on as directed by your Intelligence Filter. All you need to do is agree on a code between you and your Intelligence Filter. Hold the pendulum as you did in Step One. Close your eyes. Ask yourself "Which way is yes?" Wait for a motion, opening your eyes, every few seconds to check it out. Keep asking the question until you perceive a motion. It might be subtle at first, but it will get more and more pronounced. Once you get a consistent motion, then that is the motion that will be the code for "yes." Now ask, "Which way is no?" Again wait for consistent motion. You now have a motion for "yes;" perhaps it is side to side or to and fro, and a different motion for "no." You still have two motions left and two more code responses to set up: "I don't know" and "I won't tell." The latter is an escape hatch for the Intelligence Filter in case the information might be harmful for you to remember, as when the mind causes amnesia.

When you have successfully completed these two steps, you will never have to go through them again. You are ready to use the pendulum to identify causes of illness.

To help you formulate the sequence of questions that lead to the pinning down of the causal event, here is a typical sequence that Bob could have used to get at the cause of his upsets and vomiting.

Question	Pendulum Motion
Was the cause present over ten years ago?	No
Over five years ago?	No
Before my marriage?	No

Over two years ago?	No
Over one year ago?	Yes
Is my diet the cause?	No
Is my business the cause?	No
Is a person the cause?	Yes
Is my wife the cause?	No
Is it my mother-in-law?	No
My father-in-law?	Yes

At this point Bob exclaimed, "Aha!"

The realization of the cause usually comes through in no uncertain way. Bob realized that since his father-in-law was the cause, it had to be the quandary into which his father-in-law was putting him with constant pressure to go into the stockbrokerage business.

When the answer dawns, using the pendulum, you know it. If there is any doubt, try more questions.

The sequence should first narrow down the time element, then the situation involved, then the person involved. If there is still any doubt as to how the situation and person are causing the problem, further questioning is needed.

Once the cause is identified, use the Autogenics procedures described in subsequent chapters to defuse the cause.

Meanwhile, use the following enhanced mood and relaxation formula and applicable change formula to alleviate the symptoms.

Three Autogenic Steps for Alleviating Disease Symptoms

We are now going to set forth three simple steps to get rid of the unwanted symptoms of a number of serious health problems.

What mood formula do you use? What relaxation formula? What change formula?

The mood formula for relaxation—the one about being in a peaceful place—is always a good one to use. But setting the mood for good health, when absence of the best of health is the problem, is better.

You can set the mood for good health by picturing yourself in top health. It is better not to go backward in time to remember yourself without the symptoms, but instead to go forward in time and see yourself free of the symptoms.

What would your tomorrow be like without this sickness? See yourself rising in the morning and going about a vigorous, productive, fun-filled day free of any semblance of the health problem.

That is a powerful mood-setting formula for a return of good health. Daydream in this manner for a minute or two and you will be ready to start the next step—the relaxation formula.

The enhanced relaxation formula is the same as you experienced in Chapter 2 plus an additional portion devoted to better mental and physical well-being. But instead of your remembering the basic procedure, listen to the relaxation word for word. Have somebody read it, or tape it yourself.

Start your friend reading or start making the tape with the indented material on page 36 in Chapter 2. Stop before the words "In a few moments you will count to ten."

Then insert the following indented material. This will complete your health relaxation formula. When the tape ends, you repeat your change formula and count yourself back to "wide awake," one to ten.

Here is the added relaxation material.

> You feel a pleasant, wonderful drowsiness. It is almost the feeling you have when you fall asleep. A similar feeling, a similar sensation, just as when you fall asleep. And as you continue to relax and as you continue to feel some of the heaviness, some of the drowsiness, you will also feel comfort. In fact, you will become so comfortable that you'll have no desire to move. No desire to think of anything, no desire to do anything. For every day now, your nerves will become stronger and steadier. Your health will improve. You will have more energy. You will become so deeply interested in whatever you are doing. So deeply interested in whatever is going on, that your mind will become much less preoccupied with yourself. And you will become less conscious of yourself and your own feelings. You will feel more comfortable. You need not have any desire to move or to speak. You need only a desire to relax. You are relaxing, your body is becoming very relaxed. You need not have any desire to move at all, only a desire to relax, deeper. And not only can you relax now, but you will find that you will always be able to relax. Whenever you think of relax-

ing, you can find the feeling of relaxation. Whenever you want to relax, you will always be able to relax. You will find every day that your mind will become calmer, clearer, more composed, more placid, more tranquil. And you will feel better physically. You will become less easily worried, much less easily agitated, much less fearful, much less apprehensive, and much less easily upset. And you are becoming even more relaxed now. You are becoming drowsier now. You want to reach the deepest possible state as it will be so beneficial to you. And all the suggestions you hear will be completely effective. As I count now, I'm going to count from 1 to 5, as I do so, you will be able to sink into a much deeper state, and at the count of 5, you will feel the depth of the state. You will feel how much more comfortable, how much more relaxed you have become. Now, I will start counting. 1, feel yourself sinking much more deeply. Deeply into the state of relaxation. Further and further away from any outside concerns. Just enjoy where you are and what you are doing. 2, each number carries you down deeper, with each word I say. With each moment that passes, you're able to drift deeper and deeper into this state. 3, deeply, soundly. You can feel yourself sinking into this wonderful, comfortable state in which you pay attention to nothing else. Nothing else need concern you, nothing at all. 4, as I continue to speak to you, you drift deeper. All the suggestions that I give you will be totally effective. From now on, you will be able to think more clearly. You will be able to concentrate more easily. You will be able to see things in their true perspective without magnifying or distorting them. Without allowing them to get out of proportion. Every day you will become emotionally much calmer, much more settled, much less easily disturbed. Your body will respond and you will feel better. You are becoming more and more relaxed and more and more responsive to these words. You are becoming more and more responsive to these instructions. And every day you will have a greater feeling of personal well-being. A greater feeling of personal safety and security. More than you have felt for a long time. Every day you will become and remain more completely relaxed both mentally and physically. And as you become and as you remain more relaxed and less tense each day, so you will develop much more confidence in yourself. From now on you will have much more confidence in your ability to do not only what you have to do each day, but also much more confidence in your ability to do whatever you ought to be able to do without fear of failure. Without unnecessary anxiety, without uneasiness. And every

> day you will feel more and more independent, more able to stand on your own feet no matter how difficut or trying things might be. And because all of these things will happen exactly as you now hear that they will happen. You already are feeling more relaxed about your health and your progress. You are going to feel much happier, much more contented, much more cheerful, much more optimistic. You will be much less easily discouraged, much less easily depressed. You now feel the peacefulness and the benefits of deep and profound relaxation. You will be able to enjoy the benefits of this relaxation in everyday life. You will find yourself calmer, more relaxed, more composed and more confident, much more healthy and youthful.

Once you have gone through the daydreaming about a healthy you and relaxed deeply using the tape or a friend, you are ready to apply the change formula.

I now provide change formulae for a number of different health problems. Look them over even though they do not apply to you. In this way, you see the common thread that runs through them all so that you can create a change formula for any disease. Of course, if the disease that troubles you is listed, you are ready to proceed affirming to yourself the change formula before ending your relaxation by counting one to ten, opening your eyes, feeling great.

Arthritis. The discomfort in my ________ diminishes daily. My ________ can move freely and without discomfort. I project good health and I see myself well.

Asthma. My breathing is relaxed. The shortness of breath is less and less intense. Every moment I breathe more and more normally. I see myself inhaling and exhaling so comfortably and without strain.

Colitis. My inner discomfort is diminishing. My whole digestive system is normalizing. I see myself becoming able to digest food easily.

Dental problems. The sensitivity and pain in my mouth and teeth are diminishing. My teeth and gums will become healthy and strong. I expect wellness and I see myself well.

Diabetes. The blood sugar cycles of my circulation normalize with each passing day. My pancreas supplies insulin as needed. As I recover, I will need less and less medication and my body will normalize. I expect full recovery.

Gag Reflexes. My mouth and throat become more and more relaxed. I can feel them relaxing. My mouth and throat are normalizing I see myself not gagging.

Gastro-Intestinal Disorders. My entire intestinal system is relaxed and calm. I feel better and better. My stomach and intestines are normalizing. I project wellness and I see myself fit and well.

Hysterical Distress. I am becoming more and more calm. I am more understanding of myself and others. I restore peace within. I feel more and more in control. I create peace. I see myself confident and peaceful.

Menstrual Distress. I free myself from past memories of menstrual distress. I approach my next period relaxed and expecting more and more freedom from distress. The cramps become fewer and less intense. I expect freedom from menstrual cramps. I see myself free.

Rheumatism. The discomfort becomes less and less. I no longer expect to have the discomfort that occurred in the past. My (insert area) is becoming totally free of pain. I feel I am able to move easier. I expect wellness and I see myself well.

Skin Problems. The skin on my (insert area) improves daily. The blemishes become less and less. The old skin cells are replaced with new. My skin tone improves. My skin becomes more and more radiant and attractive. I see my skin healthy and unblemished.

The Next Step Is Up to You

You cannot improve your health merely by reading this book. You now have the Autogenics equation for good health:

Mood formula + Relaxation formula +
Change formula = Restoration of good health.

Reading this equation is not enough. You must apply it.

I hope you will go through these three equation steps. First, arrange for a reader or make the tapes. Review your mood formula. Practice repeating the change formula applicable to your problem so you are able to repeat it to yourself. The words you use can be your own as long as they cover the same ground as supplied above.

Repeat your Autogenics sessions daily—even two or three times daily if you have the time—until the condition has improved.

Remember, Autogenics is not a substitute for care by your physician. It is a supplement to it. Help your doctor help you with Autogenics.

In the subsequent chapters, we leave physical health problems and get into living a better life. We begin the process of improving our happiness, our fun, our finances, and our success.

CHAPTER 4

Autogenic Protection Against Stress

IN THE PAGES that comprise the rest of this book, we leave the area of health and get into the area of well-being.

To live better you need to know how to defuse past unwanted conditioning; programming and habits; to insulate yourself against present unwanted stress; and to program yourself for greater future efficiency, skills, and accomplishment.

You now have the basic routine to follow to get rid of fears—from fear of insects to fear of public speaking. You have the basic procedure to control sexual problems, anxiety, neuroses and personality quirks. You know the three formulae of Autogenics which you will you will learn how to apply to end doubt, impatience, boredom and confusion.

You will learn how to apply them to get rid of excess pounds or excessive smoking and other unwanted habits. You will learn how to apply them to increase your creative ability, athletic ability and everyday skills, such as sewing, typing, and gardening.

There is no end to the application of these simple formulae to solve daily problems and we will go over specific applications for attracting members of the opposite sex, for turning failure into success, and for accumulating more money. "Impossible" situations and "insoluble" problems dissolve with the power of your mind as you apply Autogenics in directed ways.

That is the thrust now of this chapter and the chapters that follow. As you use Autogenics in the ways described, you get out of ruts, acquire a winning personality, and attract love, wealth and admiration of all those whom you meet and work with.

We begin in this chapter with handling stress, particularly the stress caused by fears and phobias, but also the stress caused by threatening situations.

These situations are fearful and threatening because of a basic feeling of inability to cope with them, a feeling of distrust in ourselves.

How Trustworthy Are You?

Did you know that Einstein was four years old before he could speak and seven before he could read? Isaac Newton was another scientist who did poorly in school.

The famous inventor Thomas Alva Edison, when a boy, was told by his teachers he was too stupid to learn anything.

Caruso was told by his music teacher, "You have no voice at all." Another famous singer, Madame Schumann-Heink was told by the director of the Imperial Opera in Vienna that she would never be a singer and would be better off if she bought a sewing machine.

Leo Tolstoy flunked out of college and rocket expert Werner von Braun flunked 9th grade algebra. Louis Pasteur was "mediocre" in chemistry, according to Royal College where he studied.

Did you know that Winston Churchill failed the sixth grade; and that Abraham Lincoln entered the Black Hawk War with the rank of captain and came out as a private?

What all of these people received in the way of criticism and rejection would be enough to cause most of us to retreat to a life of mediocrity. We would accept the stamp of inferiority and we would proceed to live it out.

Not so the great people mentioned above. Their greatness was derived largely from a decision: I will not accept the failure image. I trust my own ability.

We all have 30 billion brain neurons. None of us has been shortchanged. The difference is in what we accept for ourselves.

A person who accepts limited capability becomes a frightened, insecure shadow of his true self. He is racked with indecision, anxiety, phobia and distrust.

For such a person, life can be hell. And there can appear to be no escape from its suffering. If you are not one of these people gripped by fear, you have no idea what they go through. If you are one of these people, you are probably saying it is even worse than I describe.

There is a way out.

When you change your mind, you change everything else.

The famous people I have just mentioned experienced low points, too. They thought in terms of limitation when limits were thrown in their face by others. But they changed their minds. They made a decision against such limits. They had a deep down trust in themselves.

"Yes, but ..." Who said that? If you said it, you are mouthing a cop-out. "I tried." "I'm different." "It didn't work." More cop-outs. Think failure and you are doomed to failure. Think success and ...

Finish the above sentence. Say it aloud. Believe it. Create a climate for you to change your mind about yourself.

If you could stand in my shoes for a few days, you would see peoples' lives change as they changed their minds about themselves.

There are 700 known phobias and one of the most common is the fear of being alone. We have seen that so many times in our offices—people who are absolutely terrified of being alone. So it was with Harriet. She told me that the first seven or eight years while her husband was sick, she had developed a fear of being alone—of her husband dying and leaving her. A few months ago her husband had died and she was alone. Now just as she feared, her life was terrible. She tried to do things, to be with people, she tried to invite people to her apartment, anything but to be by herself. And the worst time was at night. She could not seem to face the dark and lonely nights.

More recently, she had begun to take tranquilizers and sleeping pills. At the beginning they seemed to be helpful. Now they seemed to have no value at all. Yet, she still continued to take the medication because she was afraid that without the medication she would feel even worse.

I asked Harriet to put her goal into words. It took her quite a little while to analyze what her goal was. In the end, she said, "I just don't want to have that feeling."

"What feeling is that," I asked.

"I don't know how to describe it," she replied. "It is just a terrible, terrible feeling. I don't want to have that feeling."

Did she have any objection to reaching the goal? No. Could the goal become a reality? With some hesitation the response was "yes." I gave her Autogenic ways to allow the Intelligence Filter to produce the effect that she wanted—to produce the effect that she would no longer have those "terrible" feelings.

She called me about five or six days later, and she said that she was still getting feelings, but they weren't as bad. But something else had happened. She had suddenly decided to sell her apartment and move to Florida. And that, in fact, she was going to Florida that weekend to look at a condominium in a community in North Miami and that she would call me in a couple of weeks.

When she called me, she said that she had sold her apartment quite quickly and had taken the condominium. She wrote to me some months later from Florida. She had made a number of friends there. In fact, she had met a gentleman who she felt might be her next husband. The fear of being alone was virtually gone. She had never thought of selling her apartment and moving away, but somehow she seemed to be driven to doing so. She informed me joyfully that she was about to take golf lessons and was looking forward to her new life.

The Intelligence Filter works in wondrous ways. We are geniuses. When we permit our minds to function without the limitation of indecision, cop-out and self-immobilization, the "terrible" feelings are wiped out in genius-like ways.

What a Phobia Really Is

What exactly is a phobia? It is any *unfounded* or morbid fear or dread. In other words, if you break out into a cold sweat every time you set foot on a boat, you are phobic,. However, you would have been perfectly "normal" if you panicked on the Titanic.

If you hate to be stared at (scopophobia) or panic at the thought of being alone (autophobia), you are among the millions of Americans suffering from one of the more than 700 phobias that have now been identified.

The most common phobia is believed to be claustrophobia (fear of closed spaces). Both Presidents Kennedy and Roosevelt shared that particular fear. The most disabling phobia is thought to be pantophobia (fear of everything), while the most recently categorized phobia is logizomechanophobia (fear of computers).

A partial list of phobias would include:

Acrophobia	—	Fear of heights
Agoraphobia	—	Fear of open places
Ailurophobia	—	Fear of cats
Androphobia	—	Fear of men
Anthropophobia	—	Fear of people
Apiphobia	—	Fear of bees
Bathophobia	—	Fear of depth
Ceraunophobia	—	Fear of thunder
Chromophobia	—	Fear of certain colors
Decidophobia	—	Fear of making decisions
Entomophobia	—	Fear of insects
Ergophobia	—	Fear of work
Gephydrophobia	—	Fear of crossing a bridge
Gynephobia	—	Fear of women
Hydrophobia	—	Fear of water
Iatrophobia	—	Fear of doctors
Mysophobia	—	Fear of contamination
Nyctophobia	—	Fear of night
Ocholophobia	—	Fear of crowds
Pathophobia	—	Fear of disease
Pyrophobia	—	Fear of fire
Sitophobia	—	Fear of food
Verbophobia	—	Fear of words
Xenophobia	—	Fear of strangers
Zoophobia	—	Fear of animals

The Decision to Change Gives Birth to Change

Your name is probably not Harriet. Your fears and anxieties are undoubtdly quite different. But they, too, can disappear in a few days, as did Harriet's, and possibly in ways that you or anyone else could predict.

It all starts with a decision.

Because you are reading these pages, you have already begun the decision-making process. You are only a few pages away from completing that process and effecting a major release from "terrible."

Sometimes self-limitation evokes fear that are as all-embracing as Harriet's. Other times these fears come only at special times.

Here are some of those 700 catalogued phobias:

Fear of high places
Fear of the dark
Fear of small rooms
Fear of elevators
Fear of appearing on stage
Fear of flying
Fear of insects
Fear of dirt
Fear of meeting people
Fear of dogs

People with these phobias experience the same "terrible" feeling that Harriet did, but only at certain times—when the fear trigger appeared.

For Pat it was when she was on stage.

Pat wanted desperately to overcome the awful disablement of stage fright. She was presently in the chorus of a Broadway musical. That did not bother her. But now she had the opportunity to do a solo in a local club. This was something that she had always wanted to do, but now that she had the opportunity, she was terrified. She was afraid she would forget the words of her songs, shake, and that her voice would choke up and that people wouldn't like her.

In the chorus, she had no such problems, for she was surrounded by others doing exactly the same as she was doing and the spotlight was not on her. But now she was going to be on her own. I asked Pat to use Autogenics and request from her Intelligence Filter a change formula that would be best for her, one that would help her reach her goal: to perform skillfully on stage. After going through the mood formula and the relaxation formula, she formulated an image in her mind. There she was in the theatre—in the audience, watching the stage, watching the curtain rise. But as she was herself walking onto the stage, it wasn't as a singer—it was as an actress. An actress who was playing the part of a singer. She created a character for herself as a confident, talented entertainer, which she could accept. Interestingly, she never did accept herself as a singer, but she did very well indeed, accepting herself as an actress who was playing the part of a singer.

One week later, she opened in the club. She called me the next day saying that she received a great reception. Some weeks later, on New Year's Eve, she did even better. The audience called her back for two encores. She seemed completely free of her old fear and anxiety. Now she eagerly awaited the next time that she was due on stage.

In this chapter, I am going to provide you with a mood formula for protection against the stress of your fears or phobias. This mood formula will set the stage for your freedom from these paralyzing events.

You will use the same relaxation formula provided in Chapter 3. But I will provide you with a change formula that is targeted for your specific fear.

We begin with the mood formula.

A Mood Formula That Brings Relief from the Stress of Fear

You know what your life is like now, plagued as you are by that fear, phobia, or stressful anxiety.

You know, too, what your life could be like free of this torment.

In a moment, I am going to ask you to put the book down and do something that will begin this new life, free of that fear you have.

What you will do will be to daydream for a few moments in a special way.

I want you to imagine you are strolling along a peaceful country lane. As you admire the natural beauty, you come to a fork in this lane. You have a choice of taking a lane that goes to the left or one that goes to the right.

As you look up the left lane, you see your life unfolding as it would be if you suffered from this fear or phobia. It is not pleasant. As you look down this lane, you see all of the torment that you would experience because of this problem. It is a painful way.

As you look up the right lane, you see your life as it would be if you were free of this suffering. It is a joyful release. You see yourself happy and able to do what you want, free of restricting fear. You see your life as you want it to be.

Next, you see yourself making a decision as to which fork you wish to take. And you see yourself stepping off down that lane, as you end your mood formula.

We will call this the two-path mood formula. It will have additional applications in the chapters ahead as we address other problems where a decision is the first step.

How to Call on Your Intelligence Filter for Help

Hypnotists and hypno-therapists are constantly seeking better ways to help their clients. They attend symposia, conventions, and professional meetings, often traveling many miles in order to attain new approaches and new techniques.

I have found that one of the best sources of the right approach lies in the client's own mind. Pat's mind gave her the actress image which proved much more effective for her than some standard approach which I might suggest.

You can call on your Intelligence Filter to come up with the right change formula image for you. It is easy to do. In fact, you do nothing. You get out of the way and let it happen. Here is how.

After you complete the two-path mood formula, turn on your relaxation tape prepared in Chapter 3 or call on your helper to read that relaxation.

While relaxing, ask your mind to give you the proper corrective images for you to accomplish your goal. Specify what that goal is. For example: "I want to know the proper picture to eliminate my fear of high places."

Then, forget about it, and continue to enjoy the relaxation reading or tape. For some, the correct image pops into the mind while still relaxing a few minutes later. But it does not have to happen that fast. You will complete the relaxation formula and then begin the change formula. It is then that you will be using the correct positive image that is just right for you.

It is best to accept whatever positive image comes to mind without questioning it. Your mind knows best. Remember, I said positive. Your Intelligence Filter will not deliver a negative programming to you. It wants only the best for you. A negative image could only be *you* waiting to suffer more. This could indicate that you need to reinforce your two-path mood formula by going through it again and re-starting your relaxation.

The positive image that you find percolating into your conscious mind can take several forms:

1. You might see yourself in a typical fear-triggering situation (elevator, plane, etc.) totally free of anxiety, relaxed and comfortable.
2. You might find yourself going through a little playlet of some kind which involves other people—a kind of psychodrama that finds you acting out a situation which bears on your problem.
3. You might picture only a first step that leads to the problem situation, such as putting on your bathing suit if fear of the water is involved, or packing your suitcase if fear of flying is the stress-causing event.

Let's examine each of these.

The first is a complete change formula. If that is what your Intelligence Filter has delivered, use it as is.

The second may be a first step. After you go through the playlet or psychodrama, you might then find you are desirous of using a mental picture, such as the first: a picture of yourself in the situation with no more fear. Your next step would then be to enjoy that success picture.

The third is your Intelligence Filter's way of saying you need to go one small step at a time.

This is known as desensitization. You desensitize yourself of fear in particular situations by exposing your anxieties to yourself little by little.

This requires a number of Autogenic sessions. Each one desensitizes you a bit more. Each successive picture you hold takes you more into the fearsome situation. If you visualize that picture without any feelings of anxiety, then you are ready for the next.

I repeat. There should be no feelings of anxiety as you put on your bathing suit in your imagination, or pack for a flying trip, or do whatever the first step might be to plunge you into a stressful event for you. If you do feel anxiety, you have taken too big a step. Backtrack and use an image that is a simpler or more preliminary one.

Do not proceed to a further image, say going to the beach, or to the airport, or to wherever your stressful event takes place, until the previous image has been pictured without a trace of anxiety.

Each step of the way should be satisfactorily accomplished without anxiety before the next step is attempted. Here, for example, are the types of stages involved in desensitizing a fear of flying:

1. Packing for the trip
2. Driving to the airport
3. Clearing the check-out counter
4. Going through security
5. Waiting for boarding at the gate
6. Boarding the plane
7. Being seated and fastening your seat belt
8. Taking off
9. Observing the view from flying altitude

You might wonder why so many steps are needed to desensitize a phobia. It is like untying a knot. It needs to be unraveled one snag at a time. Otherwise, you might only make the knot tighter.

Visualizing and living these steps in a quiet, serene, composed way is actually a reconditioning of your behavior little by little. Too big a jump and you "spin your wheels." When you feel any anxiety at any stage, it is because it has been too big a jump. You need to backtrack a stage and take it more slowly.

Gordon was the art director of a large cosmetics company. Part of his job was to give presentations to both small and large groups. But Gordon had a morbid fear of speaking in front of these groups.

Gordon was in his early forties. His appearance was crisp and professional. So he managed to hide his fear from his superiors. But for how long? He spent his days contemplating his impending doom. He was sure he would be discovered as inadequate, that he would lose his job, and that he would be humiliated and totally embarrassed. Before his presentation, his mind would become overcome with an accumulation of these fearful thoughts, feeding his phobia.

These fears had prevented him from seeking a higher position within the company. He sought help but traditional methods of psychotherapy failed. He wanted to be able to express himself in front of groups with a feeling of comfort and security. This was his target point, his goal and the reason he sought our help.

I taught Gordon the finger levitation method for obtaining answers from the subconscious as he seemed to prefer this to the use of the pendulum. We will go over this method in a future chapter. His finger levitation response was excellent, but when he was asked whether or not his Intelligence Filter was ready to proceed to the target point, there was a negative response. We then talked about this negative response. Suddenly, he described a scene that he was visualizing on this theatre stage, a technique I will describe in a moment.

He said, "I saw myself in my classroom. I believe it was my fourth or fifth grade. My teacher asked me to stand up and to answer some questions about the preceeding lesson she had given. I believe it was a geographical question. I had not been listening to her and I made some stab at the answer, but obviously my answer was not only wrong but stupid. The children around me broke into laughter and so, for that matter, did the teacher. I stood there ashamed and embarrassed. I could feel the blood rushing to my face. I was completely devastated.

"I remember, after that, that whenever we had lessons in school, and the teacher called upon various pupils to stand, that I sat there cringing, hoping and praying that she would not call upon me. It's so strange—I had never thought about that until now."

I explained to Gordon that that was the pathway his mind had always taken. But was he now ready to find a new pathway, to find a new direction. He immediately agreed. He continued with the process. He repeated that his Intelligence Filter could again investigate the cause of the problem and resolve the problem so he could create a new pathway to the target point. Gordon's mind accepted this premise.

He was able to see himself talking to larger and larger groups and able to feel comfortable with those images on his "theatre stage." He gave himself positive "commands." He is now able to speak to groups. He is no longer disabled. He is becoming more and more comfortable and has totally overcome his problem.

About the theatre stage. If you have difficulty seeing pictures of yourself in various stages of progress, create an imaginary stage and see yourself as an actor on the stage.

In addition to this disensitization part of the change formula, there also needs to be a final positive statement to "seal the bargain."

How to Word-Change Formula "Commands" for Sure-Fire Results

You set the mood with a two-path scene.

You play your relaxation tape or listen to it read.

You start your change by picturing yourself changed, or, if that causes stress, by picturing yourself making small changes toward the target or goal.

Finally, you assert the goal as if it were already achieved. These are "commands" to your mind for altered behavior. Your mind obeys.

You end your Autogenics session.

Let us go over these commands. How do you word them?

You have already seen these "commands" spelled out for various specific ailments in Chapter 3. At the conclusion of this chapter, we will spell out these commands for a number of specific fears.

But first, here are some general principles that apply:

Be positive. Do not use words like "may" or "could." Do not use commands that suggest to yourself you may be able to do something or perhaps you could do something. Be positive and absolute, knowing and believing completely and without doubt that you can achieve the result. Doubting suggestions or doubting commands bring only doubtful results.

Be simple. Use as few words as possible in short complete sentences.

Be direct. The words should confront the problem directly. General ideas, such as "I will be a better person," do not produce as measurable results as specific ideas, as, "I will be a better typist."

Use pictures with words. Pictures should still be used while making commands. They could be the same pictures you used at the beginning of your change formula, or they could augment and elaborate on those pictures.

For example: If you have always become flustered while making a speech, your suggestions might be: "I will be relaxed while speaking. I see myself as a competent and interesting speaker. I am composed and at ease while I speak. The audience relaxes me." While making these suggestions, you must mentally visualize yourself speaking to the audience—relaxed—confident—interesting—composed—and at ease.

Even if you follow these wording instructions to the letter, you can undercut your own success. The key is attitude.

Importance of Attitude While Making Changes for the Better

Bill, a twenty-year old bachelor, although intelligent and physically attractive, had been very shy since his early childhood. He had retained the same friends, two or three of his childhood friends, but did not make new friends. He had had only one job since he left school and his social life was restricted to the same places, same people. He ate in just one or two restaurants. He turned down all invitations to new places, and as time went on he became more and more fearful.

After a while he developed anxieties about things that might produce physical harm. He became afraid of airplanes, trains, bridges, elevators. He would travel and cross the bridges but with greater and greater anxiety. The goal that he sought when he came to me was self-confidence. He wanted to feel safe. As he progressed with the exercises that I taught him, he seemed to take less notice of other people's opinions. He, in fact, was beginning to stand on his own two feet.

But his own attitude toward himself still left much to be desired. He went through his Autogenics with a feeling of resignation. I felt he was doing me a favor and did not really expect his life to change by it. Still, he admitted that people had told him he seemed to look more composed and more assured and he was also become more adventurous and less afraid—trying some new things. But nevertheless, Bill never did become really adventurous. He did improve, but he kept that improvement within bounds.

I didn't see Bill for some years and when I met him again and we sat down and talked, he told me that he had changed his job, that he was now married, had a two-year old son, and that he felt somewhat better about himself. He seemed reluctant to admit even that.

I don't think Bill will ever become really outgoing. I think perhaps that the changes that he made were all the changes he could make. Perhaps later in life he will make some more strides—if his attitude changes.

There are three fundamentals about your attitude that must be present in order for Autogenics to be as effective as it can be:

1. *Belief.* You *must* believe the suggestion you are making can be realized. You *must* believe that what you are attempting to accomplish is possible.
2. *Expectation.* When you make a suggestion, you *must* expect it will produce the effect you are attempting. If you suggest you cannot lift your arm, you must *expect* or *anticipate* it will happen exactly that way.
3. *Desire for Change.* You must have an intense desire for the change you are trying to produce. You must be self-motivated for the desired change. You must be willing and anxious to commit yourself wholeheartedly toward your intended goal.

How do you change attitude? Certainly Autogenics cannot be used to change a negative attitude if that very attitude stands in the way of success.

You might say that a change in attitude on your part is largely my responsibility. In fact, that is the purpose of this book. By sharing with you the successes of other people, I hope to convince you that changes in your life are not only possible but sure. With the methodology provided on these pages and a "shoring up" of your expectation and belief, your desire for change becomes more immediate in nature. You are not only willing to "put the book down now and do it," you just can't wait to do it.

Dentists have always been conscious of the fear factor in their patients and have taken a variety of steps to allay these fears. Some dentists use soft music to soothe fear-frazzled nerves. Other decorate their offices in soft colors to make it appear different from the traditional dentist office. Equipment is masked. Murals and paintings feature mountains, seascapes, or other tranquil scenes. Plants and mobiles are used to distract patients' attention from the tools of dental work and to calm anxiety. Some dentists engage the patient in a soothing conversaton before beginning the work, seeking a topic that puts the patient in another setting—away from the probe and the drill.

All of these steps work to a degree. That degree depends on the past experiences which the patient has had in the dentist's chair. If these are fearful experiences, the attitude contains expectation and belief for more fearful experiences in the dentist's chair despite the tranquil decor. That is why dentists have not confined their work to that decor but are constantly seeking new equipment to minimize pain and discomfort. Only in that way will the expectation and belief prevail that dental work will not be painful.

Your expectation and belief need to be success-oriented. You need to be looking for every sign of success as you proceed.

Change comes gradually. If you concentrate on the problem areas that still remain unchanged, your expectation and belief become impediments instead of facilitators. You work against yourself.

Some of us are so set in our ways that we think it would take a miracle to change them. Still, Autogenics works these miracles if you are willing to see them once they arrive.

Not all of us are willing to accept a miracle.

You remember the story of the man who owned a strange dog that could walk on water. He was afraid to tell anyone about his dog for fear that they would think he was crazy. One day he invited his neighbor to go duck hunting. When a duck was shot and fell into the pond, he ordered his dog to "fetch!" The dog scampered across the top of the water and brought back the duck. He looked at his neighbor's face. There was no sign of any surprise.

When this happened a second time with still no reaction, he asked his neighbor, "Didn't you notice something strange about my dog?"

"Yes," replied the neighbor. "Can't swim."

Expect a miracle.

Autogenic Commands That Bring Miraculous Relief from Stressful Fear

Your final step in the change formula is to add a command that your mind accepts—a command that contradicts the fear and replaces it with ease. You then end your session as explained before.

Here are specific commands you can use for specific fears. If the fear that distresses you is not included below, read over these commands anyway and construct a few sentences that conform to the approach used. See the thread of similarity that runs through all—the affirmation of comfort and enjoyment.

Fear of heights. "I find that heights are part of life. I can visualize heights without fear. I can feel safe and at ease in all normal experiences. I feel positive about my safeness."

Fear of closed spaces. "I am totally aware of how large and safe the room really is. I can come and go as I please. I am comfortable and assured in any area, large or small."

Fear of people. "People add to my life experience. I gain in broadened understanding and new perspectives by meeting new people. I have a deep feeling of self esteem. I can be comfortable with anyone."

Fear of insects. "Insects (or rodents, bats, etc.) fear me. I am in complete control. I am master over such lower forms of life. I can accept the reality that these things exist but cannot harm me."

Fear of strange places. "I will be motivated to expand my life and enjoy new sights. I enjoy being in new places and new situations. I can always be myself and be relaxed and at ease where I am."

Fear of disease. "I am convinced that my body is immune to most diseases to which I might be exposed. I see myself healthy and have a positive self-expectancy of vital health."

Fear of the dark. "I accept darkness as part of normal life exposure. I am fully relaxed in any place, be it light or dark."

Fear of performing. "I am oblivious of the audience. I can comfortably focus on one or two people at the rear. I am totally at ease and confident and able to concentrate fully on my performance."

Fear of dogs. "Most dogs are friends. They express themself by barking and moving. Dogs are affectionate and loyal. I can visualize myself associating with dogs without fear."

Fear of elevators. "Elevators are inspected regularly and are safe. I can use them confidently. I can step into an elevator and feel relaxed and know that I am participating in life."

Fear of flying. "I am totally confident in the safety of planes. I know that they are the safest form of travel. I am relaxed and comfortable while flying and enjoying the experience."

Fear of new foods. "I am willing to broaden my taste sensations. I am willing to be more adventuresome while dining. Variety in foods contributes to a well-balanced diet and can enlarge my life experience."

CHAPTER 5

Autogenic Control of Anger, Depression and Other Personality Quirks

"IF YOU ARE ANGRY, take a deep breath and as you exhale count to ten."

How many times we have heard that advice. It is good advice. But it corrects the symptom, not the cause.

In this chapter we look at the causes of anger, depression and other consistent but unwanted attitudes and feelings that influence our behavior in an uncreative way. We do so not from the point of view of "my mother-in-law makes me mad" or "my job depresses me" but rather from the point of view of ourselves as the cause.

We analyze and correct the programming that makes us react with anger or depression or frustration or anxiety. Some of this programming can also cause us to react in ways that result in sexual frigidity or impotence. We can develop misconceptions and neuroses. We can wallow in insecurity and inferiority. We can develop personality quirks which can alienate our coworkers, friends, and family.

It is heartbreaking to see capable individuals succumb to the simplest of life's problems and "go down the drain" when only a few minutes a day of reprogramming through Autogenics could halt and reverse the human calamity.

There is nobody as "lost" as the person who drifts away from us on that fog-shrouded sea called depression.

The Keys to Ending Depression

Depression seems to be a growing epidemic. Most psychiatrists in the United States agree that the highest percentage of their cases falls under the general heading of depression. I remember a lecture I once attended where a student asked the professor, "What is depression?" and he answered, "When a person has no future, he is depressed."

It is difficult to know why some people who seek help for depression are depressed in the first place. Many of them have a good social life, good family life, enjoy their jobs, yet, nevertheless walk about in a constant state of depression. It is as though they have no enthusiasm for life and can see nothing good happening to them. They see no future.

Mark was one of these people. He had been taking tranquilizers for years. He didn't know what he was depressed about but walked around in a depressed state day and night. He was certainly no fun to be with. At age 28, he had a good job, but nothing in life sparked his interest. He would spend hour after hour in front of the television set, watching anything that came up on the screen. It was his escape.

He lived with his mother in a small house in Westchester and was employed as a clothing manager in a menswear store, close to where he lived. He had a variety of fears and anxieties and had, from time to time, visited psychologists and psychiatrists and had taken the est program, all to no avail.

Frequently, he tried to go out, sometimes to a bar, to a disco or tennis. But he found no interest anywhere. In fact, he would walk out with a feeling of relief and hurry home to sit in front of his television set.

He had a healthy interest in women—but was afraid to attempt to date and face possible rejection. This served to depress him even more.

A young lady suggested he come to our office. His goal was to be confident and self-assured. But even as he stated his goal, he was unsure and critical of his ability to reach it. However, after some Autogenics, he began to change. For example, he specifically noted his feelings—and analyzed them. When he felt depressed, he tried to determine why. What had happened? Why did the happening change his mood so drastically? He began to deal with each occurrence as a separate event. He no longer anticipated failure all the time.

Mark has remained extremely shy. He is still apprehensive about new things, but he is now coping with life—one thing at a time—no longer experiencing feelings and letting those feelings intensify without tracking them down and doing something about them. He no longer needs tranquilizers to deal with his existence. He is no longer depressed. He realizes there is a future.

We are now going to examine what adaptations we might need to make in the Autogenic mood, relaxation and change formulae in order to use them to handle the kind of problem with which Mark was faced.

The Many Faces of Stress

You are assigned to a United States embassy. It is your first overseas assignment. You have always wanted to be in the diplomatic corps. It is a pleasant, responsible position. You enjoy sightseeing in the foreign country where you are now stationed. What a way to "work."

Then one day, armed militants attack the embassy. You are placed into custody as a hostage. The good life becomes a life in prison. Every day could be your last. This is stress at its worst. What do you do?

Richard Queen got multiple sclerosis. It is not easy to get multiple sclerosis. Many more times people get headaches, ulcers, or arthritis from stress. When he was released July, 1980, after over eight months of stress, the MS symptoms, which had been causing paralysis and interfering with his eyesight, suddenly began to recede.

Remove stress, and you remove the cause of most physical and mental problems.

On a scale of 100, designed to measure stressful life events, the death of a spouse is rated 100 points. Getting married is rated at 50 stress points. Even Christmas can be stressful to many people and is rated at 12 points.

The Blue Christmas Syndrome has been known to put people in the hospital. Formerly married persons, now single as a result of divorce or death of the spouse, are particularly susceptible. Psychologists note that anybody who has lost his or her traditional support system can be acutely stressed during family holidays when the sights and sounds trigger memories of what could have been and act as reminders of the change that has taken place.

Distress is stress. When it is prolonged it can lead to fatigue, depression, exhaustion, despair and, if not resolved, even mental and physical breakdown.

Traditional advice given by physicians to help cope with stress include:

- Working it off by physical exercise like running, walking, playing golf or tennis.
- Talking it off to a friend, family member or clergyman.
- Helping it off by doing things for other people. Getting your mind off yourself eases distress.
- Traveling it off by leaving your troubles behind and taking an interesting cruise or trip abroad.

One thing *not* to do is use self-medication. Liquor, pills and drugs can only make the matter worse while delaying the resolution of the underlying problem.

Non-traditional advice: use Autogenics.

How to Use Autogenics to Attack Depression

If you could assign a temperature to anger, it would be hot.

Depression, on the other hand, is cold. To set the mood for ending depression with Autogenics, your mood formula needs to include warmth.

As a prelude to the relaxation formula, your mood formula will now entail a relaxed feeling of warmth. You will make your arms and legs warm and you will then make your solar plexus warm. To aid in this process, it is helpful to have a flashlight handy.

By imagining your hand to be warm, you can actually create a degree or two difference. In the Menninger Clinic at Topeka, Kansas, it was found useful for people with serious headaches to imagine their hands to be getting warmer. As this was done, thermometers registered a full two and three degrees rise in hand temperature. This was caused by more blood flowing to these extremities. As more blood went to the hands, less blood coursed through the veins of the head, reducing the pressure that was causing the headache.

As you think "warm," you will be creating the warmth you imagine. The extremities need this warmth more than other parts of the body, just the way the top floor in a steam-heated building does not always get its share. Once these extremities are heated, you will then do the same for the solar plexus, said to be a center for "feeling," for example as when we refer to "gut feeling."

The flashlight will help to convey the idea of a warming feeling. You will place the flashlight on your lap, shining first on your left hand and then on your right as you warm first one hand and then the other. You will place the flashlight on the floor pointed first at your left foot and then at your right foot as you warm up your feet. Finally, you will shine the flashlight on your abdomen as it rests on your lap, warming the solar plexus.

Once you have used the flashlight in this manner to aid with the concept of warming, you will no longer need it in your mood formula. But it is helpful to begin with.

I am now going to give you a mood formula to create warmth. It is long enough to warrant your enlisting another person to read it to you. This person can also, then, assist with the flashlight by shining it on the appropriate point. Or you can make a cassette tape as you did with the long relaxation formula, which incidentally, you will be using again in this chapter to provide you with the second phase of your three-formulae Autogenics approach to ending anger, depression and other personality problems.

If you make a tape of this warming mood formula, your procedure will then entail your changing tapes in the midst of your session. Have the relaxation tape handy so that you do not have to get up from where you are seated. Opening your eyes and changing the tapes will not interfere with the process. But getting up and walking around can cause you to lose the beneficial effects of the mood formula.

Here, now for the purpose of having it read to you or making a tape is the mood formula to be used for the personality problems covered in this chapter. Sit comfortably, palms down on your thighs. Position the flashlight to shine on your left hand.

A Warming-Up Mood Formula

"The flashlight is shining on your left hand. You feel your left hand responding to its light. It is a warm feeling. Your left hand is beginning to enjoy a sense of warmth. I want you to sit comfortably in your chair and relax. Now, look down at your left hand. Examine it very carefully. Be as sensitive as you can to whatever feelings, whatever sensations, you can notice in your hand. Relax your hand as much as you can and as you relax it, you will notice certain things happen while you relax it. And I want you to concentrate on all the sensations, all of the feelings, whatever the feelings are, especially the feeling of light and warmth. Perhaps you may feel a heaviness of your hand as it lies perfectly relaxed on your thigh. Perhaps you can feel the warmth of your hand as it rests there. No matter what the sensations are, I want you to totally observe them, keep watching your hand, notice how still it is, notice how it remains in one position. Heavy, warm. There is a tingling warmth in your fingertips. This warmth floods your hand."

(Now change the flashlight so that it shines on the right hand.)

"The flashlight is now shining on your right hand. Look down at your right hand. Feel your right hand responding to its light. Again, it is a pleasant warm feeling. Your right hand is now enjoying a sense of warmth. Be sensitive to this warmth. Again, the light and warmth flood your fingers. Your hands are warm, limp, and relaxed. Enjoy this warmth; feel it getting into your wrists. Both hands are completely warm and the warmth is spreading to your wrists and forearms. It is a glowing sensation of warmth. You welcome it; and encourage it. Feel your hands, wrists, and arms warm. Feel the warmth all the way up both arms, all the way to your shoulders."

(Now place the flashlight on the floor shining on your left foot.)

"The flashlight is now shining on your left foot. See it lighting up your left foot. Feel the light as warmth. Feel your left foot responding to the light by getting pleasantly warm. Warmer and warmer. I want you to concentrate on the sensations of your left foot. Make it warm. Feel it responding. Enjoy the feeling of warmth as it permeates your left foot."

(Now reverse the position of the flashlight so that it shines on your right foot.)

> "The flashlight is now shining on your right foot. See it lighting up your right foot. Feel the light as warmth. Feel your right foot responding to the light by getting pleasantly warm. Warmer and warmer. The warmth of both feet is now spreading to the ankles. Feel the warmth in your ankles. Feel the warmth rising into your legs. Move the warmth up to your knees. Feel both knees becoming comfortably warm. Feel both thighs responding. Your left knee and thigh are warmer. You feel the warmth. Your right knee and thigh are also warmer. Both legs, from toes to hip, are now delightfully warm. Both hands and arms are now delightfully warm. It is a pleasant feeling. You enjoy the feeling of warm arms and legs."

(Place the flashlight on your lap, pointed upward at your abdomen. You may lean it against your abdomen.)

> "The flashlight is now shining on your solar plexus, the area just above the navel. You feel the light as warmth. Your solar plexus is getting comfortably warm. You enjoy the feeling. It is a feeling of well-being. You feel it get warmer and warmer. As your solar plexus gets warmer and warmer, you feel good inside. You welcome the feeling. Your warm arms and legs and solar plexus give a feeling that all is right. You feel safe and secure."

As you close in on depression, anger, inferiority, feelings, neuroses and sexual problems that frequently derive from these problems, we need to be reminded once again of the basic procedure:

Step One. Experience the above mood formula as it is read to you or listening to your own voice on a cassette tape.

Step Two. Experience the relaxation formula the same way. This is the one previously prepared for a reader or for tape.

Step Three. Apply the specific change formula which will be supplied in the following pages of this chapter.

Creating a Change Formula to Cope with Depression

Louise had been digesting regular doses of Valium for the past six years. It was the only way she could get through depressing, hopeless days. She saw nothing in her future except further bickering and aggravation. Her husband had long since acquired a life style that she detested, leaving the house at 7:00 a.m., returning at 6:00 p.m., dinner at 6:30, snoozing until 10:00 and then to bed. Hardly was there any variance to this pattern. In recent years their sexual life had been almost non-existent.

They had two children, Harry, age eighteen, and Frank, age nineteen. The children had been a source of constant concern and anxiety—drugs, police, family conflict and frustration. Louise had no further control over their actions and their father had long since given up the battle. Louise was depressed and frustrated. There was, according to her, no silver lining—nothing she could look forward to.

I asked Louise what she had worked at before she was married. She told me that she had been a secretary, but had not worked since her marriage twenty-one years ago. We decided that we would start off with a primary target point of relaxation and attempt to diminish the stress so that at least she could deal with the things she had to deal with in a more relaxed manner. Louise was able to relate to this and after a few weeks, she found that she could relax sufficiently and diminish the amount of Valium that she was used to taking. She soon discarded the Valium completely and noted some improvement in her ability to cope with life.

Not long after, she called me and told me that she was going back to school. She was going to brush up on her secretarial skills, and was going to look for a part-time job. I encouraged her to do so. She did, in fact, return to school and later found a part-time job in a small jewelry company. Within a year she was in full-time charge of the office. She enjoyed the challenge and the opportunity and the independence.

There were some changes at home, too. Unfortunately, Harry and Frank continued with their life styles and the accompanying problems, but her husband began to pay Louise much more attention. She discussed her day at the office with him. Louise's mind and her life had taken a new pathway. She was no longer on Valium, no longer depressed or hopeless. Louise had a future.

When you do the warming-up mood formula, followed by the relaxation formula, your warm, relaxed feeling will be the kind of feeling that helped change Louise's life. When you add specific instructions to your mind for positive change, the clouds disappear and the sun comes out.

Typical change formulae that sweep away the clouds of depression involve the use of such words as stronger, more courageous, more confident, more cheerful, more composed.

These words effect change. Say them now and there is a feeling of hopelessness that they will effect a change. But say them after your mood and relaxation formulae have taken effect and no such feeling of hopelessness will ensue. Instead, you will have a warm, relaxed feeling about the whole session. Indeed, you *will* have more courage; you will be more confident and cheerful; you will be more composed.

I am going to give you 16 statements that produce these changes. Select one, two or three—as many of them that seem to be right for you as you can comfortably remember.

Say them over to yourself at the termination of your being read to or the tape. Then count yourself up and your will feel the difference. Read them over now. Select the ones that fit. Remember them and you will be ready for your depression-ending Autogenics session: OC 2

- I see things in positive dimension and true perspective.
- I am less preoccupied with myself and more positive about my dirction.
- I know that self-motivation produces achievement, success and happiness.
- Everyday I become more positive and more self-assured.
- I am calmer and more composed, my goals are within my grasp.
- I can create a positive self-image and be confident.
- I no longer allow myself to be apprehensive or upset.
- I am less and less easily discouraged. I know I will be able to do whatever I set my mind to do.
- I am free of unnecessary guilt and self-contempt. I have a positive self-image and positive self-expectancy.
- I enjoy life and feel optimistic about the future.
- My nerves are stronger and steadier, able to deal with life as it comes.

- I work with self-discipline and self-control.
- I am gratified with each positive step.
- I always remember to target myself to be cheerful and happy.
- I will appreciate the efforts of others and use their help to achieve my goals.
- I am mentally relaxed and eager and ready to grasp opportunities.

In repeating the several statements you select, be sure to see yourself the way you describe. Mental pictures that go with the words help to reinforce the results.

How to Cool Down Anger with Autogenics

Stress can move us in many directions, as we previously discussed. The same set of circumstances that drives one person to deep depression can drive another to heights of anger.

So it is not the set of circumstances itself that is the problem. It is the way you react to it that may be a problem. For many people that same set of circumstances would spell no problem at all—no depression, no anger, and no negative personality defect in between.

Tensions are not always bad. Tensions are a natural part of life. They play a useful role in life. If hunger did not cause a type of stress or tension, we would not eat. If thirst did not cause physical stress or tension, we would not partake of liquid so necessary to the survival of our body. If there were no sexual tensions, the survival of the human race would be left to chance.

Without the ability to be tense, we would not be able to handle emergencies and to overcome situations that could be harmful to ourselves or our families.

Those of us who enjoy competitive sports, either as spectator or participant, are exploiting tension. We use it as a stimulating experience. Often that stimulation which starts out as pleasure can be converted into anger. Fights break out on the field or in the stands.

It is this moment in time that needs to be addressed. What converts constructive emotions into destructive emotions?

Helen was an angry person. She was referred to me by a friend of mine who was a physician. She had gone to see him because she complained that she was tired all the time. She feared that she had something wrong with her stomach because she continuously had pains there. The physician had examined her quite extensively and could not find anything wrong.

When I spoke to Helen, she told me that she felt that she was taking life much too seriously. She had become very serious over everything. She was continuously worried about her health, she was restless, tense, unable to relax, she complained that she was unable to concentrate, that she lost her temper frequently and had difficulty making even the simplest of decisions. Her temper and periods of anger left her remorseful and depleted.

Helen's case was by no means unusual. She seemed to have all of the symptoms of stress. I spoke to her physician and asked him for his opinion. He felt that stress was probably the reason for Helen's condition.

Helen seemed to be one of those people who are affected by even moderate amounts of stress. Even as a child she had tended to push herself too hard, always trying to overachieve, always making demands on herself that taxed her capacity. As she grew older, she made these demands more frequently. Eventually, the fatigue and the anger began to take their toll.

Helen's target point seemed to be quite obvious. It was coping with the stresses of her life. Soon after she began her Autogenics with me, she began to make a number of changes. The changes that she made seemed to be coming from her inner mind—they were not planned changes but things that she thought came to mind after the sessions. We talked about these changes and she told me some of them. For one, she said she had stopped relying on alcohol. She had never mentioned alcohol in the previous visits. I didn't know that she drank, but evidently she did. And one of her changes was to avoid relying on alcohol. She also told me that she was now taking regular exercises. She was walking and she had taken up tennis. She also was going to bed earlier—she was getting more sleep. I did not know that Helen had been taking sleeping pills to sleep. She had told neither the physician nor me. But now she had given them up.

Another change that had taken place was that Helen became aware that she had pitied herself a great deal, and one of her new rules was to avoid self-pity. She seemed to be laughing a lot more. She was even laughing at some of her problems. She had now adjusted to making compromises when previously there was only one way to go. But now, she was not afraid of taking another pathway. Finally, she had prepared herself for conditions that she thought might be stressful. She developed a habit of writing them down and talking them over with herself. Sometimes talking them over to others who had a similar problem.

All of those solutions were in Helen's mind. The trick was to get them out—and she did. She had no further trouble with her stomach and was able to do most of the things that she wanted to do. She got along better with people. Helen was no longer an angry person.

Your inner mind knows the answers that are right for you. The way Autogenics helps is to permit them to percolate up to the conscious mind.

The solution for anger may not come in the form of specific answers as to what you need to do. But just as Helen began to make appropriate changes in her behavior, you will find yourself making changes in your behavior, too. These changes will move you away from anger as a reaction to stress and in the direction of a more constructive reaction.

The change formula for anger triggers the mind to provide these behavioral changes as answers to the anger problem. You use this formula after using the flashlight warmth formula and the taped or read relaxation formula. Then before counting yourself up to end your Autogenics session, you tell yourself:

> *"I want to know how to react positively instead of angrily to stress. I ask my Intelligence Filter to provide the means by which this can be done. I must know and I will know. My anger is ready to leave. I am ready to use reason, calmly and coolly to handle all situations constructively."*

And you end your session.

Ending Problems That Interfere with Sexual Pleasure

The many faces of stress include several that are found in bed.

Of these, the most common are male inability to have an erection, and female inability to have an orgasm. Frigidity and homosexuality are also problems common to both sexes.

These problems, caused by stress, in turn cause more stress. Each can be an energy-sapping, devitalizing condition. Autogenics can help.

Men first. Once a man fails to perform in sex—and it could be due to liquor, fatigue or some other special circumstance no longer prevalent—he may then anticipate continued failure. Anxiety is a sex depressant. By worrying about failure, a man also is programming himself for failure.

Jack was a mild-looking man in his thirties. His problem was he could not get an erection unless he play-acted he was a soldier breaking into a house and ordering a woman to undress. He then fantasized forcing the woman to submit to him sexually under threat. Since he often needed to back these imaginings up with vocalized "orders" and indeed often used stage props, all of this required cooperation by his sexual partners, which was not always forthcoming.

Years of psychotherapy failed to remove Jack's problem. When he came to me for help, I asked him to go through his little drama. Then, I asked him to go through it again while deeply relaxed. This time I had him assign numbers to each step of the drama. When he breaks into the house, number one. When he confronts the woman, number two, and so forth. When he returned for his next session, I had Jack relax and just go through the numbers slowly without playing the scene. When he got to number four (she takes off her clothes), he got an erection. Jack was then instructed to concentrate on the numbers at his next sexual encounter instead of doing the play-acting. It was an unqualified success.

You can program yourself to get an erection "by the numbers."

Remember your last successful sexual encounter in every detail. Go through your mood formula, your relaxation formula, as provided for in this chapter, and then visualize this last successful sexual event. This time, give each step a number.

Create your own steps befitting your own successful experience. Give each a number.

Go over it once again in your relaxed state. End your session.

You have now used Autogenics to get an erection. When you have your next sexual encounter, give each step a number, spacing the numbers so that when you reach number eight, it is the right time for an erection.

How the Female Orgasm Can Be Triggered

The chief obstacle to a woman's reaching a climax of pleasure in the sexual act is tension. The tension is largely due to a carryover of Victorian attitudes toward sex as sinful for a woman to enjoy. When initial sexual encounters are spoiled by this guilt feeling, there can be a carryover into the marriage relationship despite the obvious absence of any justification for grief.

Other reasons for non-orgasmic behavior in women include fear of pregnancy, fear of being hurt, fear of contracting venereal disease. All of these are tensions. When tension for any reason interferes with orgasm, then the pattern has been created for another tension: tension about not getting an orgasm, and, as in the case of the male, the problem becomes self-perpetuating.

You can reverse the cycle with Autogenics. By going through the warming-up mood formula and the taped or read relaxation formula from one hour to a few hours before the sexual event, the stage is set for a tension-free act.

Seal the bargain with a simple change formula:

> *"The relaxation I feel now will return to me when I engage in love-making. I will be blissfully relaxed."*

Then you end your Autogenics session by counting yourself up in the usual manner. And let nature do the rest.

Sometimes women's troubles begin before the sexual act. A woman can have no desire to engage even in the foreplay that precedes the sexual act. This is similar to a phobia and can be alleviated by the desensitizing method used in Chapter 4.

The classic application of this is the case of the woman who had a fear of the male sexual organ. This was, of course, interfering with her marriage. Her therapist had her go to a museum and stand 50 feet from a nude male statue. Each day she was to return and stand a few feet closer. If there was any anxiety felt, that meant she had rushed the process and would have to start over in smaller increments. When she was able to stand next to the statue without anxiety, she was then instructed to touch the genital area. Next, she was to repeat the process in her living room with the cooperation of her nude husband, standing closer and closer until she could touch his parts without anxiety. Finally, in small increments, the physical contact of the sexual organs was approached until the sexual act itself could be undertaken without anxiety.

We find that imaging the above sequence in the privacy of your own living room while relaxed produces the same effects as trips to the museum or encroaching on the husband's time. Small mental steps desensitize the sexual phobia just as well.

If you are suffering from sexual frigidity, you can attack it head-on by creating a scenario to visualize your progressive, step-by-step change formula. Or you can go back in time and identify the cause by using your button-on-string pendulum.

With the pendulum, you can ask a range of questions calling for a yes or no answer that covers all the possibilities you can think of—low metabolism, phobia, childhood experience. Once you identify the cause, your change formula will write itself.

You put an end to the frigidity by understanding what caused it and undoing the connection. (''Uncle Bill's exposure to me is in the past. I forgive him. The experience no longer effects me today. I am free of it.'')

Homosexuality, Neuroses and Other Personality Defects

Sexual attraction to members of the same sex can derive from physiological causes or it can be mentally acquired.

We will not suggest Autogenics if the problem lies in the genes, although there have been cases where behavior has been altered through therapy. Nor will we suggest Autogenics where the status quo of homosexuality is accepted and no change is desired.

However, many homosexuals, especially in initial stages, desire a change from this behavior. For them we recommend a series of sessions with Autogenics that utilize the warmth mood formula in this chapter, the read or taped relaxation formula, and a series of visualized changes as part of the change formula that go from disinterest in the same sex to passionate attraction to the opposite sex.

If progress is not evident, then the use of the pendulum to identify a causal event might be needed. When the event is identified and understood—this includes a forgiveness of the party or parties involved—then the causal event is defused. You are then able to go back to the visualization sequences as change formulae with a greater likelihood of success.

Phobias and anxieties and neuroses—functional disorders of the emotions—involve abnormal behavior symptoms. Many neuroses could exist that are not evidenced as phobias or anxieties. However, these should be not confused with psychoses which are severe mental disorders that are characterized by deterioration of normal behavior—intellectual and social-functioning—and a partial or complete withdrawal from reality.

Persons with a psychosis or in a psychotic condition should seek the help of a professional therapist.

Persons with a neurosis or neurotic condition can help themselves with Autogenics, although here, too, the advice and supervision of a therapist is recommended.

It is an oversimplification to say that all neuroses can be handled in the same way. But most personality quirks and defects will respond to the methods contained in this chapter and the previous chapter.

- Use the warmth mood formula.
- Use the relaxation reading or tape.
- Use the sequential images that desensitize.
- Use positive statements to trigger the change.
- End your Autogenics session.

You can use any one or several of the positive statements that were listed earlier in this chapter. Or you can use or add some of the more specific ones listed below, if they "zero in" on your problem:

- "I am in control of my life and my emotions."
- "I am a capable and attractive person and see myself growing and achieving."
- "This is a universe in which order prevails and in which I can take an exciting place."
- "I am confident in my role as a (man, woman), and of my direction."

- "I am self-disciplined and optimistic."
- "I am safe, strong, and happy."
- "I will conscientiously make myself secure about the future."
- "I feel warmth and understanding toward others and communicate with others."
- "I refuse to think negatively—I replace all negative thoughts with positive direction."
- "I enjoy my own company. I can feel unity and oneness."

Do it. The time involved is small compared to the great new life that awaits you.

CHAPTER 6

Autogenic Ways to Peace of Mind

WE ALL SEEK PEACE OF MIND.

Brief detours from peace of mind are welcomed, as a suspense novel, a basketball game, or a half-hour with the evening newspaper. But prolonged periods of suspense, indecision, or conflict deprive us of a deep-seated hunger for peace of mind.

We have already provided with Autogenics the means to dispose of some chief deterrents to peace of mind: poor health's stressful fears and phobias; depression, anxiety and neuroses.

In this chapter, we address some of the everyday problems that interfere with peace of mind. These are the passing events which can make living either a problem or a pleasure, depending on how we relate to these events.

Autogenics can help us handle events that would otherwise cause grief, confusion, boredom, indecision, impatience or nervousness.

When we use Autogenics to handle such events, we reduce these negative reactions, perhaps eliminate them completely; and substitute peace of mind in their place.

Would you like to be successful in business? This is a common goal for many people throughout the country. My co-author, Dr. Stone, is a volunteer counselor for the U.S. Small Business Administration. He sees countless people striving to get started in business who are faced with problems that contribute to confusion, impatience, and indecision. I see scores of these people too, in my practice.

Take Leonard.

He was a widower. He said that indecision was plaguing him. Spin-off attitudes included depression, frustration and instability. Here is his story.

When Leonard met Maria, he was working as a general manager in a food processing factory. Maria had a small catering business where she would go to people's homes and cook and serve for small parties.

They did a lot of traveling and after eleven years of marriage, Maria became ill and shortly thereafter died from a rare blood disease.

During the time of their marriage Leonard often had helped Maria in her small catering business. His role was one of a general aid—cleaning up, taking care of the dishes, and sometimes helping with the cooking. After Maria died, Leonard continued to work in the plant and, from time to time, would receive calls from people who wanted small parties catered. In most cases they did not know of Maria's death. Leonard, working with an assistant, would take care of these parties and so, for a number of years, he held both jobs, factory manager and caterer.

When I first saw Leonard he told me how tired he was—that the two jobs were really too much for him. He was in a general state of depression and frustration. He said that what he would really like to do would be to build the catering business and to give up his other job. But he didn't feel that he had the ability to build it and make a living from it. Leonard's income at the time was about $35,000 a year, of which about $10,000 came from the catering.

I asked Leonard whether or not his target goal was to become successful in the catering business. He paused for quite a little while and then said, "Yes it was." I asked Leonard to sit back and make himself comfortable and that we were going to see whether or not we could achieve that goal. He seemed quite enthused at the prospect of ending his indecision.

After Leonard was sufficiently relaxed, I asked him whether or not his Intelligence Filter would agree to work toward the goal. I watched his finger for the signal yes in a way which you are going to learn in this chapter, but I did not get the signal yes. I asked Leonard whether or not there was a blockage.

"Is there something preventing you from responding positively?" His finger raised yes there was.

"Do you know," I asked Leonard, "what it is?" There was no response from the finger, meaning no I don't.

I asked Leonard to allow his mind to investigate the blockage and to clear it, and to signal to me when the blockage was cleared. Leonard raised his finger immediately. For the moment I thought Leonard had not understood the suggestion, so I repeated it. Once again, the finger immediately responded. I asked Leonard whether or not his Intelligence Filter could now put things in place for him. He responded, yes.

I instructed then that things would be put in place and that he would signal to me when this task was completed. It took one and a half or two minutes. Eventually, he responded that the task had been completed. We then terminated the session.

Leonard looked at me and said, "You know, I have a feeling now of what I have to do. I have to put myself into this job. I have to visit people. I have to call up all of our old customers and ask for referrals. I have to print some business cards and work out some menus. I have to look for more efficient help.I have a feeling that it is going to work out."

I showed Leonard how he could reinforce the sequence that we had used in the office. How he could ask himself the questions and get the responses. How he could self-direct, simply by repeating the same sequences I had used when he was in my office. And I asked him please to call me in a couple of weeks and tell me how he is doing.

Leonard did not call me in a couple of weeks—in fact, about three months went by before I heard from him, and not through a telephone call in the office, but at a party that I went to which Leonard was catering. When he saw me he seemed somewhat ashamed, and he said, "I'm sorry—I've just been too busy to get around to calling you." He told me that the effects had been remarkable, that he had completely lost his frustration, indecision and depression, that he was totally enthused in his work, that he had seemingly found abilities he never knew he had possessed and that his company, now grown to sixteen people, was a success. He felt, for the first time in many,

many years, that his mind was clear and that his future was safe and assured.

And that's what peace of mind is all about.

How to Get Valuable Signals from the Deep Recesses of Your Mind

The kinds of problems that interfere with peace of mind, which we are addressing in this chapter, require a mood of readiness to let them go, a mood of acceptance of your own efforts to change.

You cannot force this readiness or acceptance. But you can encourage it and induce it.

The mood formula we will use involves the raising of your index finger as a positive indicator of this readiness on the part of your mind to relinquish the problem and move in the direction of resolution and inner peace.

If the finger does not rise in response to your question, the mind is not yet ready. You can then use the finger response to see what steps are required to initiate that readiness.

To estabish communications between your mind and your index finger requires a one-time session. The words for this session will be provided now. It can be read to you or you can make a tape with your own voice. You will not need the reader or the tape again after this one session. You will have established the connection. Your index finger will rise, as did Leonard's, when you relax and ask your mind a question about a peace of mind problem.

Some people establish this finger levitation quite easily. In fact, they do not need the long session I am about to provide. You might want to check out your own finger levitation susceptibility before using the longer method. Here is the short method. There are two steps:

> *Step One.* After you have read this, close your eyes, put the book down, and do it. Extend both arms in front of you, parallel to the floor, palms down. Picture a heavy shopping bag over the right wrist. It is filled with groceries. Imagine you feel the weight of these heavy groceries. See the items sticking out of the full bag—maybe melons, detergent, other heavy items. Feel the

weight pulling down on your arm. To your other wrist is tied a red balloon. It is filled with helium and is pulling up toward the ceiling. Feel the tug upward on your left wrist and the weight on your right wrist. Open your eyes and look at your arms. If they are no longer parallel to each other, you are ready for the next step.

Step Two. In this step, you begin by sitting comfortably, taking a deep breath and as you exhale relaxing your body. Your hands are on your lap palms down. You become aware of your hands. Feel their weight on your thighs. Feel their warmth. Be sensitive to a difference in weight. Does one hand feel lighter than the other? One will feel lighter if you focus your awareness. As soon as one hand feels lighter, concentrate on that hand. Feel how sensitive this hand is to your clothing on which it is resting. Whatever sensation you feel in this hand, concentrate on that sensation. Now transfer your attention to the index finger of that hand. Feel those same sensations there, especially the lightness. The index finger is extremely light. Now imagine your lap is an old-fashioned scale. Your heavy hand is on one balance. Your light hand is on the other. This causes your light hand to rise. Feel this inclination to rise in the index finger of your light hand. You know this finger will rise. You feel it pressing less and less on the leg. This concentration causes a nerve impulse. The index finger rises. It may take a few seconds of concentration or a few minutes but it will rise. As it rises, repeat to yourself several times, "This rise of my (left/right) index finger means yes." Then open your eyes.

Read over Step One. Then put the book down and do it...
Read over Step Two. Then put the book down and do it...

An Alternate Method to Institute Finger Levitation

If you attained the desired response, there is no need for you to read this section. You are ready to proceed to use this finger levitation mood formula to obtain agreement from your mind for ending boredom, grief, nervousness and similar obstructions to peace of mind.

If you did not attain a finger levitation by this method, prepare for a longer exercise involving assistance from a family member or friend who will read the following passage to you; or involving your making of a cassette which you will then play back as a one-time exercise to inaugurate finger levitation as a yes signal from your mind. Here is the passage.*

I want you to sit comfortably in your chair and relax. Place both hands, palms down, on your thighs. Now, look down at your left hand. Look at it very carefully. Be as sensitive as you can to whatever feelings, whatever sensations you can notice in your hand. Observe the color of your hand, the feeling of your clothing on your hand. Relax your hand as much as you can. As you relax it, you will notice certain things happen. I want you to concentrate on all the sensations, all of the feelings, whatever the feelings are. Perhaps you may feel a heaviness of your hand as it lies perfectly relaxed on your thigh. Perhaps you can feel the warmth of your hand as it rests there. No matter what the sensations are, I want you to totally observe them. Keep watching your hand, notice how still it is, notice how it remains in one position. There is really movement in your hand. Soon this movement will become noticeable to you. I want you to keep watching it. Keep watching your hand. Even if your attention wanders from your hand, bring your mind back to your hand. Keep watching it and wonder within yourself when the motion will show itself. This motion will take place in your index finger. Now focus your mind on the finger next to the thumb of your left hand, the finger next to your thumb. This is your index finger. Soon, that finger is going to move. Keep watching it and you will begin to notice a slight movement; and as the movement begins, you will notice that very slowly the finger will begin to lift, will begin to lift up. It will begin to lift slowly and the space between your finger and your thigh will slowly widen. This will be the signal from your mind that "yes" you are ready to relax deeply. Now, as soon as you see the finger moving, as soon as you see it make even the *slightest* movement, I want you to voluntarily close your eyes. So, as soon as you see the finger moving, as soon as you see it lifting or making the smallest motion, I want you to immediately close your eyes. This will be the signal that you are ready to relax. Your finger is becoming lighter, you are becoming aware of a feeling of lightness in your finger, as if it feels like a feather, as if a balloon was lifting it up and up in the air. Lifting, lifting, lifting the finger up and up and

*This passage assumes you are right-handed. Left-handed persons should look at their right hand, not the left.

up; lifting it up, pulling it up higher and higher. This lifting of your finger is your mind's way of signaling yes. In the future whenever you ask your mind a question, it will signal a "yes" answer by your left index finger rising, "no" by its not rising. "Yes" by rising. "No" by not rising. I will now count from one to ten. At the count of ten you will open your eyes feeling wide awake and at a high level of well-being. One, two, three, four, five, six, seven, eight, nine, ten!

You do not have to go through this session again. It has done its job. It has established a simple way for your mind to agree to change. You will get a rise of your left index finger (right index finger for lefties) when your mood is one of readiness for a change.

If your finger does not rise when you sit down for an Autogenics session and ask the question "Am I ready to end my grief?" or whatever the unwanted state of mind is, then you can ask additional questions about the matter so you can identify what you must do before you are ready. More about that line of questioning later in this chapter.

Turning Indecision into Decisive Goal Achievement

Lisle worked as a computer programmer. He worked for a large company and was very good at what he did. His company had recently merged with another and Lisle was offered a job with considerably more pay if he would go out and sell computer software and, at the same time, help program those companies who purchased his goods.

Although it meant an increase in pay, Lisle was apprehensive about his sales ability and giving up the comfort and safety of the job he had held previously. This apprehensiveness plagued him day and night.

His company was insisting upon a reply to their offer, and Lisle had been procrastinating for months. The longer he procrastinated, the more fearful he became of going out to face prospective buyers and facing a possibility of rejection which he did not believe that he could deal with.

We had some difficulty in establishing a goal because Lisle felt that the only reason he was contemplating this new job at all was because of the pressure brought on by his company and his wife who thought that this was a great opportunity and did not understand why Lisle was not jumping at it. I asked Lisle for a finger response on this question: "If you could go out and sell your products without the feelings of fear and anxiety that you now have, would you like to do that?" His finger replied yes. I asked Lisle to comment on that inner response. He replied, "I certainly would, but I would not like to do it if I was uncomfortable and I hated every day of it."

We discussed what his anxieties were. He basically feared failure. He feared rejection. He had a poor self-image and he lacked confidence.

I asked Lisle whether he had the knowledge for the job. He immediately replied affirmatively. For awhile we discussed his goal. I asked him to ask his Intelligence Filter what the basic goal should be. Lisle suddenly said, "I want to make my goal 'I can.'"

"What do you mean by that?" I asked.

"I mean that my goal is, I can, I can do anything that I set my mind to."

After Lisle had been taught the methodology, and just before he left the office, he turned around to me and said, "You know, there is more to life than having your basic needs satisfied."

The end of this story is quite interesting inasmuch as Lisle did accept the new position. He did well in sales. Although he never really loved it, he was offered another job by another company, at much more money, where he did not have to do sales and he grabbed it. I believe he knows now that if he ever wants to do something, he can use his "I can" goal and do it. That certainly gives Lisle peace of mind about himself.

Notice how rapidly Lisle's Intelligence Filter came up with a clarification of his goal. Yours will, too, once you get a mood formula "yes" through a finger levitation to your question, "Am I ready to give up my.... (grief, indecision, boredom, etc.)?" The means to do it will be supplied by your Intelligence Filter.

It may come to you immediately, while you are doing the relaxation formula, or it may come to you as a flash of insight hours or days later. But it will come. If it does not come immediately, your change formula will also serve to trigger its arrival.

You will continue to use your taped or read relaxation formula, followed by the change formula which we will get to in a moment.

I am attempting to place as many do-it-yourself techniques in this book as possible. But it takes some skill to be able to ask yourself the right questions—the kinds of questions I asked Lisle, for instance, that triggered such fast responses.

All the therapists at my New York Institute for Hypnotherapy must undergo weeks of training in the Petrie Method® and all must qualify for membership in the American Association of Professional Hypnologists. This training enables them to recognize individual barriers and to evoke responses that circumvent these barriers.

Other therapists from across the country attend our staff training programs as observers to learn these procedures and many professional organizations, wishing to introduce hypnosis as part of their treatment modality, choose our method under a licensing agreement.

I wish I could train and license you to get to the recesses of your own mind through Autogenics; but a point is reached occasionally where professional assistance is required. It is always better to work with professional assistance; and even when you are your own "self-hypnotist," it is recommended that you work under professional health-care supervision. Sometimes a professional hypnotist can do what is extremely difficult for a self-trained individual to do.

I am going to give you some simple approaches to getting to the center of barriers to peace of mind and rooting them out. If you are successful, you have my congratulations, but, of course, the resulting peace of mind is its own reward. If you are unsuccessful, seek out professional assistance.

How to End Disturbing Factors and Attain Peace of Mind

You have acquired the ability to get a "yes" or "no" answer from your subconscious mind via finger levitation. If you programmed or conditioned this by the short method given, then whichever index finger felt lighter and went up when placed on the old-fashioned scale balance is the one that will now provide you with the "yes" response.

If you used the longer read or taped method to program finger levitation, then the index finger of your left hand if your are right-handed, right hand if your are left-handed, is the one that will now provide you with the "yes" response.

The use of these responses occurs in the mood formula. What you learn by the finger response is:

1. Whether you are ready to continue with the relaxation and change formulae.
2. What direction the change formula should take.

I am going to take each of several major problems and go through a sequence of possible "yes" or "no" responses, ending with the change formulae that is indicated by these responses.

It is not possible for me to cover every possible situation, but by reviewing several you can get a feeling of the process and be more ready to apply it in your special case.

The right questions for you will evoke ideas. They may come as immediate creative feelings or ideas. They may come as positive daydreaming or as imaginings. These pictures and ideas are being delivered to you by your Intelligence Filter. Try them out. Test them out. Use them. They are usually the right answer for you, especially if you pass the test of being progressive, constructive, creative and/or positive.

Old pictures that plague the mind, disrupting its peace, need to be snipped out in the motion picture cutting room and new pictures substituted in their place. Let us now look at this procedure for some typical disruptive pictures.

Grief. Sit comfortably and relaxed. Look at your index finger. Ask yourself whether you are ready to let go of your grief. "Am I ready to put aside my sorrow over (My mother's passing, my divorce, the bankruptcy, etc.)?" Wait patiently for a response from your finger. If the finger does not lift within a minute or two, I will give you some additional questions to ask. If it does lift, then you are ready for this change formula (after the relaxation formula):

"Everything happens for the best. My gloom is turning into sunshine. I face each day with joy and with peace of mind."

If the finger gives a no response by not rising, you may want to wait a few days and try again. Or you may want to pursue the matter now in order to zero in on "why?" Again, ask "yourself."

"Should I wait for a few days?"

A "yes" response would indicate that you will be wise to wait out your grief and try again in three or four days.

A "no" response—no finger levitation within a one-to-two-minute period—could be followed by such questions as:

A. "Is my grief really a type of self-punishment?"
B. "Is my grief really my feeling sorry for myself?"
C. "Is my grief really loneliness?"

Continue with this type of questioning until you hit the jackpot. A "yes" answer, once received through the rising of your index finger, then indicates the change formula to use. Change formulae for each of the above questions follow:

A. "I can end my guilt and forgive myself. The past is past. I will never repeat my mistakes. I face today with a clean slate, confident, optimistic."
B. "Self-pity is counter-productive. I will not allow myself self-pity. I face life each day having learned from the past."
C. "I am never alone. I am part of my family, neighbors, co-workers, friends."

Once you have handled the block in this way, go back to your "Am I ready?" Now you should get a yes response. You can then use the "Everything happens for the best..." change formula.

Indecision or Confusion. Sit comfortably and relax. Look at your index finger. Ask yourself "Am I ready to make a decision on this matter of (job, apartment or house, location, to do or not to do, etc.)?"

If a yes answer comes, use this change formula: "I am clear-minded. I am ready to make a decision. That decision is now at hand. I claim it."

You will *know* what to do. The decision will usually come without any lingering doubt. If you have any doubt, you can always direct a question to your Intelligence Filter: "Is this decision (state it) correct?" Wait for a "yes" finger levitation. If none, start over.

If there is no finger response to your original question, you are not ready. You can wait a few days and try again. Or, you can use more questions to identify the block. Some examples:

A. "Is my indecision (or confusion) related to matters that need to be resolved first?" (Then continue with further questions to identify these matters.)
B. "Is my indecision (or confusion) due to fear of failure?"
C. "Is my indecision (or confusion) due to an absence of advantage of one choice over the other?"

Change formulae that fit yes responses to the above approaches:

A. "I am patient and watchful. I can absorb problems with a philosophical demeanor, peace of mind and a positive attitude."
B. "I am a capable person. I am aware of my abilities. I am confident. I know who I am and where I am going."
C. "My decision in this matter is bound to be the right one. I can move ahead knowing I will make the right decision."

Now your are ready, at least in the case of B and C (for A, there is a waiting period), to ask your ready question again. If there is still no levitation of the finger, you may have to identify more blocks. If you get a "yes," proceed with the "I am ready to make a decision..." change formula.

Impatience or Boredom. If you get a "yes" response to the "ready" question, use this change formula:

"I do my best daily. I see blessing and beauty where they exist. Where none, I see a challenge to me to create them. Life is fulfilling, minute to minute."

To identify the reasons for non-readiness, these typical questions might apply:

A. "Is my (impatience or boredom) due to some particular need that I must fill?" Use more questions to identify this need.
B. "Is my (impatience or boredom) due to my reaction to some individual?" Use more questions to identify this person.

C. "Is my (impatience or boredom) due to some event that needs to take place?" Use more questions to identify this event.

When the need, person or event is identified, then use the appropriate change formula which applies to needs and people, as supplied thoughout this book. If an event must be awaited, use change formula A under *indecision*.

You are now ready to begin over and when you get a "yes" answer, use the "I do my best daily..." change formula.

Nervousness. If you get a "yes" response to your "ready" question, use this change formula:

> *"I am relaxed and confident. I am cool and calm. Unwanted events will pass. I handle myself and others with tranquility and understanding."*

A "not ready" response might require such additional questions as:

A. "Is my nervousness due to some physical lack?" Then identify it, i.e., sleep, exercise, vitamins, minerals, etc.
B. "Is my nervousness due to some irritant in my environment?" Use more questions to identify it, i.e., traffic noice, loud radio or TV, auto fumes or other odors.
C. "Is my nervousness due to some person?" Use more questions to identify.
D. "Is my nervousness due to some need I have?" Use more questions to identify, i.e., money, sex, companionship.

In the case of A, supply the physical lacks. For B, change your environment or use change formulae that make you "less sensitive to..." the irritant. In the case of C, follow the change formulae supplied in other parts of this book to handle the various needs and relationships. Then go back to that "ready" question and proceed with the relaxation formula and the "I am relaxed and confident..." change formula.

Peace of mind is worth working for. Without it, life can be torture. With it, life can be wonderful!

CHAPTER 7

How to Lose Weight Without Will Power

DIETS TAKE WILL POWER. People who are overweight do not have will power. So how can overweight people lose weight by dieting?

The answer is they can't.

That is why there are so many diets and so many disillusioned dieters.

The answer lies not in food control but habit control.

Here are the habits that contribute to unwanted pounds. One or more of these habits will be recognized by any over-weight person as theirs:

- Eating when not hungry
- Between-meals snacking
- "Sneaking" food
- Late-night nibbling
- Lack of control over certain foods (usually sweets or starches)
- "Binges"
- Constantly thinking about food
- Eating too large a portion
- Lack of confidence because of repeated diet failures
- Feelings of being out of control
- "Emotional" eating
- Compulsive eating

The Petrie Method® for permanent weight control uses hypnotic techniques for overcoming these habits. Combined with Autogenics, it provides a simple no-diet program that produces quick and long-lasting slenderizing changes. It is directed to:

- Reducing the appetite and hunger
- Avoiding constant thinking about food
- Absolute control over food selectivity
- Producing self-confidence
- Producing effective slender imagery
- Rapid and healthful reduction of weight and total charge of self
- Developing a healthy food preference
- Making the way you look and feel more important then any food temptation

Do you see any mention of calories?

It takes will power to merely count calories, not to speak of curtailing them. The only will power needed to lose weight the Autogenics way is the will power to enjoy a slender mood, a pleasant relaxation, and a stimulating change formula.

Slenderizing the Autogenics Way

Since will power is the bane of dieters, it is not surprising that Autogenics which uses no will power is the delight of dieters. They write me of their successes, adding "... and you may quote me."

"A really easy way to lose weight. I am very impressed with the program."

"I have never experienced such an immediate and continuous response to any dietary program."

"My attitude toward food has changed completely."

"I never feel weak or hungry. I am eating better and feel better."

Easy, immediate, continuous with no hunger or weakness and new attitudes, better feelings. This cannot be a diet. It must be some other change. It is.

It is a change in the person.

If you have experienced Autogenics in the previous chapters as for better health, or for more confidence, or for dissolving unwanted behavior quirks, you know that nothing else changed except *you*.

Changes in *you* are brought about by programming the servomechanism called your brain to behave you in ways that you want instead of ways that you do not want.

Once new instructions are given to the brain, new behavior is ordered by neural signals. These go out in electrical form and travel at 270 miles per hour. That means an inhibitory signal can travel from your brain to your stomach in less time than it takes to think about that quart of ice cream in the freezer. ''Cancel. Not needed.''

These signals automatically move you in the direction of nutritional foods and away from sugary and fatty foods—once you have programmed new behavior with the Autogenics change formulae.

If you think you have to be somebody special in order for this to work for you, the noise you are about to hear is the explosion of another myth and one of the more common cop-outs: The code that brain neurons use to transmit behavioral information to other parts of the body is identical in leeches, crayfish, tigers, humans.

You do not have to be any more developed than an insect for your Autogenics change formulae to be implicitly carried out. The results can be life-altering.

Take Susan, 55. She came to us the first time to get rid of her smoking habit. This she did quite easily. (See next chapter.) She came to us again quite soon thereafter because she had always had a weight problem but now she was concerned that she was turning to food as a substitute for cigarettes. With some additional instructions for using the self-hypnotic techniques of Autogenics, this too was handled.

Susan was now a non-smoker with stabilized weight. But it was not long before she returned to us for the third time. She had lost her only living relative.Her job was producing considerable competitive stress. Other events in her life, including the sex department, were putting her under such tension that it was becoming more and more difficult for Susan to remain a non-smoker, normal eater, and a composed individual.

We discussed a target point for Susan. She agreed that, instead of the target being control over smoking or control over eating, it should be control over stress. Because, if the stress factors were diminished, or, hopefully, totally eliminated, then the desire for cigarettes and unneeded food would diminish. Also, her outlook would be more optimistic and she would be a happier person.

So diminished stress became the target point, using largely the same mood formula, relaxation formula and change formula as we have already used in the previous chapters.

Susan did not return for a fourth go-around. The new programming worked well. I do not usually hold my breath in these matters or cross my fingers or watch the appointment book. I forget all about Toms and Susans as I get busy with the Jacks and Helens. I would not have known the outcome in Susan's case had she not been moved to write a year later. She had achieved permanent control over the smoking, the weight, and the state of mind. "At last I am free. Thank you."

In this chapter, we are going to emphasize target. Autogenics for weight control is less likely to consider for its prime targets, apple pie, mashed potatoes, or barbequed ribs. It is more likely to consider for its prime target a more slender self-image, a higher self-opinion, a feeling of security.

Sub-targets may also have to be handled, having to do with specific eating habits—such as eating when not hungry, eating sugary foods, overeating a particular food.

Identifying a Target Point for Your Weight Problem

Susan used her intellect to decide her target points. The intellect utilizes only a small portion of the left hemisphere of the brain. It gave her the wrong target points—smoking then overeating—in two successive tries.

You will use your Intelligence Filter. It calls on much more of your brain's resources for the answer. That answer is more likely to be dependable.

Here is how:

- First, you will set a slenderizing mood.
- Second, you will relax using your tape.

- Third, while relaxing, you will ask your Intelligence Filter for the correct target point.
- Fourth, you will use a hand mirror to encourage an answer.
- Fifth, you will write yourself a letter that will divulge the target point.
- Sixth, you will create a change formula aimed at that target point.

You will then be ready to again set the slenderizing mood, again play the relaxation tape, and finally give yourself the change formula custom built for your particular weight problem.

There has already been a change in your consciousness that will help to solve your weight problem. In fact, the solution is underway.

An unexplained phenomenon of the human mind which is used universally in therapy is: with understanding comes cure. By your developing an understanding that those extra inches are not caused by your wolfing down doughnuts and french fries but by an emotional factor that sends phony appetite signals, you are getting a handle on those phony signals.

This should come as good news to you. Just by reading the last page or two, you have developed new insight into overeating and are beginning to correct it.

If you do consider this to be good news, then there has been another change for the better in your consciousness which will further hasten a correction: your expectation and belief have been raised a notch or two.

Expectation that your mood formula will set the mood aids the mood to be set. Expectation that you are relaxing deeply deepens your relaxation. Expectation that your change formula is right on target and will cause the change you want aids success there, too.

Whether you come to me in person or read this book, it is up to me to raise your expectation of, and belief in, success. Doctors know that if they have a patient who believes he cannot be cured, he is going to be a difficult patient to cure. Some surgeons will not operate on a patient with a negative belief in the outcome. We tend to create and live out our expectations and our beliefs.

With heightened expectation of losing weight, you are now on the threshold of becoming a more slender person. You can step over that threshold now by beginning the six-step process just outlined.

A Slenderizing Mood

There is no better mood for slenderizing than seeing yourself thin.

Let me give you a number of ways to do this and you can pick the way that fits you best.

The direct picture is of you looking slender. You have no bulges, just normal lines or curves. Your posture is good. If male, you have an eye-catching physique. If female, you have an attractive figure.

You can make the direct picture more specific by seeing yourself on a scale with the scale reading your ideal weight. Or, you can see yourself wearing the size dress or suit you should be wearing.

To make these mental pictures, it might help to stand in front of a full-length mirror and refresh your memory of what you look like. Then you can deflate the picture by imagining that you are letting air out as if it were a balloon.

Irma, 42, was getting nowhere with her Autogenics. After her third visit to my office for reinforcement, I thought we'd seen the last of her 30 pounds of extra baggage. But she came back a fourth time, desolate that she had made no progress.

"I guess I just can't see myself thin," she said, her voice reflecting her feeling of futility.

It gave me an idea. I went into my private office and found her "before" picture which I occasionally request for my records. I took some of my secretary's typewriter correction opaquer and whited out a portion of her silhouette. Then I showed her this picture of her slenderized self. She looked at it a moment. Then tears rolled down her cheeks.

It was a breakthrough for Irma. She lost steadily and became that picture.

The mind can picture anything you have a mind to picture. If you cannot picture spinach maybe you have "something" against spinach. Face up to that "something." Admit it is there. Decide it is not valid. Release it. Lo and behold: an image of spinach.

You can do the same with an image of yourself with unwanted poundage on your frame.

To set the mood, sit quietly in your relaxation place, your cassette tape ready to be turned on. Have a hand mirror next to you.

Close your eyes. See yourself slender. Use the scale or the clothing size or full-length mirror image. Then daydream about what a difference it will make in your social life or your sex life or your job—or all three. See yourself looking younger, feeling better, being more energetic. See admiring eyes on you. See yourself the life of the party or the "star" of the beach.

Now turn on the relaxation tape. Or, if you have a helper, have that person read the relaxation monologue that begins on page 36.

"What Is the Cause Behind My Excessive Weight?"

As you relax deeper and deeper, you are going to ask a key question of your Intelligence Filter. The answer you receive to that question may drift into your mind. You will think you are making it up. Recognize it as a possible answer to the key question you have asked. Remember it, but at the same time be open-minded to more information, as there may be several aspects to the answer.

The question to ask your Intelligence Filter is "What is the basic cause behind my overweight?"

Relax. Ask the question. Be aware of what pops into your mind.

Lillian, 53, supported 180 pounds on her five-two frame. She had high blood pressure and other health problems. She had been married to a good husband for 30 years, and her four children were now grown and out of the house. But during most of this marriage, her mother had lived with her up to the present day.

It was easy for Lillian to identify the one irritant in her life: her mother. "There is no way I can describe my mother. She is everything—a troublemaker, sarcastic, intelligent and beautiful even now." Lillian said the most painful part of her daily life was staying home with her mother. So she visited a lot. And wherever she visited, she ate.

Lillian used Autogenics to lose weight, yes, but she also used it to get a "divorce" from her mother. She programmed that her mother's problems were not her problems. She programmed to toss them right back in her mother's lap.

In six months Lillian had gone from 180 pounds to 125. Her blood pressure was down and her general health was improved. But more than that, she was able to cut the umbilical cord so to speak. She was insulated from her mother's trouble making. In fact, she was insisting that her mother find her own apartment. Case closed.

Anthony, 35, came to us at the recommendation of his sister. "Anybody who could get my sister off her 3½ packs of cigarettes a day for ten years, ought to be able to help me with my problem." I looked at his five-foot-ten frame and guessed he was one hundred pounds overweight. (I was close—110 pounds in excess.) But his full beard and tacky clothes made me wonder if weight was his real problem.

He explained he was a salesman of software for computers. He felt his appearance worked against him. His excess weight, he feared, was a strain on his heart. He ate on the run, mostly junk foods, and was constantly snacking more of the same. He ate one real meal a day, late at night. He called it his "big dinner."

The target that emerged from Anthony's Autogenics session was to take better care of himself. He understood this to mean losing weight, dressing better, eating right and sleeping regularly.

Anthony returned a few months later for reinforcement. He had lost 65 pounds. He wanted to lose 40 more. He enjoyed being complimented on his appearance. His target point was the same. When next I saw Anthony, he was smartly dressed, clean-shaven, looking in excellent physical condition and was running in a marathon that weekend.

Your target will not be the same as Anthony's.

I am not going to give you examples right now of the kinds of answers to expect. The subconscious is often devious in its attempt to maintain the status quo and it might latch on to one of these examples, instead of delivering your own. I will give you examples later when you have gone through this procedure and are ready to create a change formula based on your own Intelligence Filter's answer to the key question.

Close by you is a hand mirror. Pick it up. Open your eyes just enough to see your face in the mirror.

Looking into the reflection of your own eyes, repeat the question, "What is the basic cause behind my overweight?" Or, you can reword it to say the same thing in a slightly different way, but aimed at the same information.

Other alternatives you can use to encourage ideas to surface:

(1) Change "my" to "your."
(2) Precede the question with "Intelligence Filter, what..." etc.
(3) Or ask, "What should my Autogenics target point for weight loss be?"

Complete your relaxation.

Before ending your relaxation and counting yourself up, give yourself the following instruction in place of a change formula:

"My Intelligence Filter will elaborate on the answer whenever I so request."

A Letter That Needs No Postage

Often when you have a dream, as hard as you try to remember the details in the morning, they elude you. In dream therapy, you are instructed to keep pencil and paper under your pillow and write down details anytime you awake in the middle of the night. In that way you capture the essence of the dream and it is there waiting for you in the morning. In fact, as you write down the essence, more and more details return.

In order to accomplish the same results with your waking "dream," you will now write a letter to yourself. And I mean *now*, that is, as soon as you put the book down and go through the mood formula and relaxation with mirror described above.

Go immediately to where you usually do desk work and begin writing. You are writing a letter to me, or your best friend (maybe we are one and the same). You are explaining how you feel when you take a second portion which you do not really need, or that second breakfast, or that midnight snack.

Again, I am not going to tell you the kinds of things to expect in the letter. You will be writing your own experiences. You may have known right along what was causing you to overeat. Or, you may have had a sneaking suspicion, a sort of lurking knowledge that has now surfaced. Or, it may all come as a complete surprise.

Whatever comes, accept it, write it down. Go into a past event if that is what comes. Detail it. Go into an emotion, if that is what comes, following it back to its source. Go into your relationship with another person, if that is what comes, living it on paper. Whatever comes, let it all "hang out."

I won't keep you any longer. I know your are anxious to cross the slenderizing threshold.

Set the slenderizing mood.

Relax, asking your Intelligence Filter for the key target, and using your hand mirror.

Write that letter.

Do it now.

Creating a Change Formula That Changes Your Weight

I hope you do not read any further until you do the steps just outlined. This is a do-it-yourself book. If you came to my office, it would not matter how much you read or do not read, because I would in effect be doing it for you or with you.

But you cannot read a do-it-yourself book on building a radio or a boat and find it all built waiting for you when you put the book down. It takes stop-and-go reading. When you stop reading, the project goes.

If you have stopped reading, and permitted your weight-loss project to go, you now have a letter that may be worth additional years of life to you. That makes it priceless—providing you stop reading and go with the project two more times before the end of this chapter.

The next stop will be to create your own special weight-loss change formula. I will tell you when. First, let's talk about it.

Are you a big business executive with the need to show off your large corporation? That can spell a 44-inch waist. Are you a lonely housewife carrying on a platonic love affair with your refrigerator? That can also spell over-sized measurements.

It has been said that inside every fat person is a skinny person trying to get out. That can be translated in different ways: Inside every overweight person is a:

A single girl who is substituting a full stomach for a full sex life; or

A single man who is seeking escape in food from the necessity of demonstrating his manhood;

A married woman who looks to food for the pleasure she is not receiving in bed;

A married man who finds diversity in dining that is denied him in love making;

A person who was shown love as a child with food and who now feels loved when eating.

Love is a powerful force in life. The above examples barely scratch the surface of love-related causes behind extra poundage. However, there are other causes.

Eating to live is creative. Living to eat is destructive. Overeating can be associated with destructive emotions.

Evelyn, a 42-year-old unmarried woman who worked in an insurance office, was gaining weight steadily. She dieted on and off and the pounds would be off and on. Evelyn did not have to be relaxed very long in Autogenics to gain insight into her problem: She was afraid of losing her job. If there was an argument or uncomfortable time with her supervisor, she would head for the coffee shop and take solace in food. Evelyn's target point became security. Her change formulae were to go from fear to self-reliance and from discord to harmony. She also went from 160 pounds to 138 in six weeks.

Fear and discord are destructive emotions. Here are some more:

Remorse	Self-Contempt	Apathy
Envy	Worry	Weariness
Jealousy	Distrust	Frustration
Hate	Pessimism	Malevolence
Anxiety	Boredom	Suspicion

Look in the letter you have written for love-related or other emotion-related causes to your eating when you are really not hungry.

A reason is there. Your own mind implores you to see it, accept it, and understand it. Your mind is programmed for your survival. Close your eyes to the reason behind your self-destructive overeating and you work against your mind and your survival.

"Not me." "I'm happy." "I'm a normal person." "I tried." "It's my glands." "I just enjoy eating." These are cop-outs.

Take a pencil right now and underline those parts of your letter that point to something. Then in the margin name that something.

Perhaps that something—that underlying annoyance—is insecurity. Then your target point is the opposite of insecurity. And your change formula must be in the direction of self-confidence and self-reliance.

By now you should know how to put a change formula into words to accomplish the desired results. Here are several examples to help you. They are chosen from the situations described on the last few pages. You word yours from your own situation as depicted in your letter.

Insecurity—"I am a complete person. I am not vulnerable to the caprice of others. I bounce back."

Loneliness—"My interest in my environment increases daily. I enjoy myself as much as I enjoy others."

Anger—"I understand others better. They do not get under my skin. I do not confuse their problem as my own. I accept others and I accept myself."

Fear of Sex—"I welcome intimate relations with the opposite sex. I am not intimidated by sex. I enjoy the affection and the sensuousness of making love."

Hunger for Love—"I am patient. I know my lover (mate) will be with me. I thrive on the memory and expectation."

Create a picture to go with the words. See yourself in a non-food setting, coping and happy.

You are now ready to repeat the slenderizing mood formula described earlier in this chapter, the relaxation formula by tape, and the change formula you have just created.

O C 4

Eating Habits and How to Substitute Good for Bad

You may not have to read any further in this chapter. You have the Autogenics tools to put out the "fires" that have fueled your appetite. The false hunger that has prompted you to eat unnecessarily has been dampened by your first corrective Autogenics session. Subsequent reinforcement sessions will continue the progress toward normal eating.

Then again, you may have to read on. If you have had a weight problem for a number of years, that is, it is not something that has been brought on in recent months, you have probably acquired some habits that will need Autogenics to end them.

Maybe you have acquired the sugar habit, and have become almost addicted to sweets.

Maybe you have acquired the fat habit, and go for eggs, cheese, cream, sauces, dressings and such meats as beef, pork, and duck more than you should.

Maybe you have acquired the snacking habit and go from second breakfast to cookies to coffee break to pretzels to whatever else is handy.

Maybe you have acquired the extra portion habit, the midnight dinner habit, or the eat-while-cooking habit.

The need for these habits disappears when you program yourself out of a negative state and into a positive state. But the habit itself may linger on.

If it does, you need to aim your Autogenics at that particular habit, or multiple habits if you have more than one.

To do this, you need to recognize the foods that give you the most nutrition for the least weight gain. Briefly stated, here they are in an approximate order of preference:

1. Salad materials
2. Leafy green vegetables
3. Other vegetables

4. Citric fruits
5. Other fruits
6. Whole grains, including whole wheat bread stuffs
7. Potatoes
8. Poultry without skin (no goose or duck)
9. Fish and sea food
10. Lean meat
11. Eggs
12. Low-fat cheese

Now here are the foods that do not deserve to be called by that name. They give your body nothing of permanence except weight They are in no particular order because I consider them to be totally out of order:

Ice cream, pies, cake, candy, soda drinks, pastry, fatty gravies, oils, butter or margarine.

In between these two lists are scores of other foods that you can eat without labeling them an unwanted food habit.

Autogenics now provides you with a way to drop the junk foods and to substitute priority foods in their place.

Make a list of the junk foods you are eating—sugary and fatty foods with practically zero nutritional value. If doughnuts are included, head the list with a picture of a doughnut—a big zero. Keep this list at your side for your next Autogenics session.

Here is your change formula: "These foods no longer serve me any purpose. They do not satisfy me in any way. I am attracted to salads, vegetables, fruits and whole grains more and more. They fulfill my needs and satisfy me."

When you have performed the slenderizing mood and the relaxation tape, do your change formula with the list in your hand. When you say, "They do not satisfy me in any way," crumple the list and throw it on the floor.

You will see and feel the difference immediately. However, some may need to repeat this Autogenics exercise every few days for a week or two as reinforcement.

Three Ways to Stop a Problem Food Dead in Its Tracks

Sometimes an eating habit connected with overweight hangs on despite the emotion target and the junk food target and despite positive pictures of a slender, attractive you.

Larry, 55, ate a quart of ice cream a day. His 240-pound, five-foot-ten frame showed it. He programmed for ridding himself of the fear of getting old, the target point that surfaced for him, but it did not rid him of the daily ice cream or the pounds.

He zeroed in next on the ice cream. He used the obnoxious technique, one of three choices I gave him. Immediately, his liking for ice cream turned to loathing. He could hardly watch anybody else eat it. For Larry, it was the end of ice cream and the end of about 40 pounds over the next two months.

Here is a suggested change formula for ice cream or whatever food you wish to wish to cancel from your regimen:

> *"I speak to that portion of my mind that goads me into eating (ice cream) despite my knowledge that it fattens my body and saps my good health. I now no longer seek momentary taste pleasure for such long range damage to my body. From now on, the taste of (ice cream) is as bad as its effects. Instead of tasting like (ice cream), it will taste like burnt rubber (or castor oil or some other bad-tasting material in your experience)—bitter, acrid, and uneatable."*

Another way to zero in on a problem food is to program a substitution:

> *"I no longer eat (ice cream); whenever I have the urge to eat (ice cream), I enjoy eating celery instead. Celery, for me, now takes the place of ice cream and is even more satisfying."*

A third way to attack a problem food is to imagine as your change formula a picture of your being force-fed that food. Let somebody for whom you have an aversion, as your neighbor, your teacher, your dentist do it in your picture. Let that person feed you in your imagination until you can almost feel yourself getting nauseous.

I hope you do not have to use these negative approaches, but when the positive approaches leave a problem still ongoing, this will handle it.

Losing weight is one of Autogenics' most gratifying rewards. Is there anybody who does not welcome better health, greater popularity, and a longer, happier life?

Special Note: A monologue for taping or reading by another person has been provided in an Appendix. It includes Relaxation and Change Formulae and is for general weight loss use.

CHAPTER 8

How to Stop Smoking and End Other Unwanted Habits

BY COINCIDENCE I began to write this chapter on the annual Great American Smokeout day, on which the American Cancer Society hoped to induce some millions of Americans to give up cigarettes for 24 hours. Last year, a Gallup Poll found that over 16 million across the nation had at least tried to make it through the day without taking a puff.

The rationale behind Great American Smokeout day is that people can do something about their habit. It is based on research that has shown smokers with the best potential for quitting permanently are those who have made one or more attempts to quit.

The rationale behind this chapter is quite different. It is based on our experience with thousands of chronically addicted smokers who are now happy and healthy non-smokers because of our methods. As far as we know, we are the country's oldest and most experienced smoking-cessation organization of its kind. A number of large corporations use our services to enable their management and employees to quit smoking—not for a day, but permanently.

Can you remember what you did on the last Great American Smokeout day? Did you participate at all? How long did you last? As you sit back now reminiscing, drawing thoughtfully on your cigarette, can you imagine yourself not wanting a cigarette? It can happen now. You can lose your desire to smoke beginning today.

This is the Petrie Great American Smokeout chapter. It is not a day. It is a chapter in your life.

Forgetting Past "Quits"—
Preparing for the Last Quit

About 80 percent of all the smokers we see have been through at least one other quit-smoking program. The techniques we use are quite different.

We do not use the aversive therapy where you are forced to smoke rapidly for long periods of time. Nor do we use another type of aversive therapy where warm, stale, smoky air is propelled in your direction. We do not use electric shock treatment, subjecting your body to a sudden change each time you are ready to reach for a cigarette. We don't have long persuasion lectures.

We use self-hypnotism with Autogenic approaches—relaxation and reprogramming—the strongest form of persuasion known to man. We support your conscious desire to quit smoking with a subconscious distaste of smoking.

It works so well that we hold regular monthly smoking clinics in many cities without advertising of any kind. Smokers arrive and groups are formed purely by the recommendations of others who have previously attended and are now non-smokers.

Have you heard about Outward Bound? It is a wilderness survival training. Once confined to youths interested in a summer activity, Outward Bound is now a year-round program for business personnel—executives, secretaries, salespeople, etc. They climb sheer mountains together with safety ropes, cross rivers on rope "bridges," rappel down vertical cliffs. When your life depends on your secretary at the other end of the rope, a sense of teamwork and self-esteem develops. The experience produces changes for the better in personal life and for the company.

Would you be motivated to spend such a week in the wilderness? Compare the motivation needed to hang from a cliff on a rope to the motivation needed to read this chapter, put the book down, then go through a few minutes of mood setting, relaxation, and mental instructions.

It's a "piece of cake" compared to other more rugged approaches. It takes less effort. It produces less discomfort. It requires less time. Don't take my word for it.

"It takes the agony out of stopping smoking," writes Hilda.

Writes Leslie, "I was amazed at the ease with which I stopped."

"I think it's wonderful," says Martin, "I have tried to stop so many times on my own and just couldn't."

"I think it is the most painless method of quitting I know," writes Herman.

And Joyce writes, "I feel as if I have never smoked in my life."

Most every habit responds to the method you will use for quitting the tobacco habit. We will emphasize smoking, but later in this chapter we will show you how to adapt Autogenics to end other types of unwanted habits, including alcoholism, nail biting, coffee drinking and others.

The Mood Formula for Beginning an End to Smoking

Light up. Be aware of how you do it.

As you puff on your cigarette, be keenly aware of the taste, the sensation of the smoke going through your throat into your lungs, and then coming back up and out.

Now let your mind review all the negative aspects of the process you are experiencing—all the factors that you already know are reasons to stop smoking. Here are some reminders, but make your own list starting with what you already know and consider most important, then adding what may come as news to you:

- The bad taste in my mouth
- The insensitivity of my taste buds for food flavors
- The harshness of the smoke to my mouth, throat, and nasal passages
- The yellow discoloration of my teeth and finger tips
- The nicotine stains on my clothing
- The room odors I create
- The burned furniture and near fires caused by my lighted cigarettes
- The coughing and phlegm from my smoking
- My fear of lung cancer and how I will have this fear and risk as long as I smoke

- The smell of tobacco on my breath and its negative effect on others
- The increasing monetary cost of cigarettes
- The social affronts my smoking causes to many
- My shortness of breath and decrease in energy—both tobacco-related
- The damage to my lungs, heart, and circulatory system my smoking causes
- The look of aging in the skin caused by smoking
- The cost in years off my life that my smoking is destined to mean.

As you ponder each fact, see yourself in a picture that fits that situation.

You may want to douse your cigarette before you are finished reviewing your list. Your Autogenics mood is set.

Your Final Step As a Smoker

OR + C

Smoking is an addiction. To break any addiction requires a deeper relaxation than is needed for the average habit or personality quirk.

For that reason we are going to add a second tape or reading to follow the one you are now using. If you have not already made a tape, now is the time to do it.

Start with the monologue in Chapter 2, page 36 that says, "Make yourself comfortable and close your eyes."

Stop before the words, "In a few moments you will count to 10." Then add the monologue that I will now give you.

You can alter this monologue to cover other addictions such as pot, alcoholism, drugs. I will tell you how later in this chapter.

The following passage deepens your relaxation for effective handling of addiction and gives you the change formula. You will find this is done in successively deeper stages with successively stronger change formulae. It includes the final count-up (shortened to 1-7) to end your Autogenics session. And to end your smoking habit.

If taping is not possible, have a friend read the combined monologue to you.

> "As you continue to relax, there is nothing that you have to do but just be aware of my voice. You do not even have to concentrate on it. Just be aware of it and feel your body relaxing

As you relax more and more, all the suggestions that I will give you will have the effect that we want them to have. As you continue to relax, and as you continue to feel the heaviness, you will also feel some drowsiness. You will also feel a feeling of comfort. You will feel quite comfortable. In fact, you will become so very comfortable, you will have no desire to move, no desire to think of anything. You will just want to enjoy the feelings that you have, and nothing will bother you. As I tell you that you are more comfortable, you feel more comfortable, and as you drift deeper and deeper, you may have no desire to move or to speak or to do anything. You need only a desire to relax, and you are relaxing. Your body is becoming very, very relaxed. You need not have any desire to move at all, only a desire to relax deeply. You will find that the feeling is very similar to drifting off to sleep, yet you can still hear me, you can hear me and ignore everything else. You are becoming more relaxed now, just as I said you would be. You are becoming drowsier, just as I said you would be. And all the suggestions that I shall give you now will be completely effective. I'm going to count from 5 to 1, and as I do so, you will be able to sink into a much deeper state; and at the count of 1, you will feel deeper, you will feel more comfortable, you will feel more drowsy. Now, I will start counting. Five, feel yourself sinking much deeper, much deeper into the state of relaxation, further and further away from all outside concerns. Just enjoy where you are, what you are doing, what you are feeling. Four, each number carries you down deeper and deeper, with each word I say, with each moment that passes, you are able to drift deeper. Three, deeply, soundly, so much like when you fall asleep, always deeper and deeper. You can feel yourself sinking into this very deep state, sinking down and down, so comfortable, so pleasant in which you pay attention to nothing else. Nothing else need concern you, nothing at all. Two, as I continue speaking to you, you drift deeper. All the suggestions I shall give to you will be very effective. You are becoming more and more responsive to my suggestions. You will continue to become increasingly responsive. Even as the time passes, even as I talk to you, you are drifting deeper and becoming more and more responsive. You will become even more responsive to all the suggestions that I make. On the next count, you will feel how much more deeply relaxed you are. One, deep, deeply relaxed. You are so very deeply relaxed now that you are able to respond completely to all the suggestions that I shall give you, and everything that I tell you, you will feel. Everything that I tell you is going to happen, will happen exactly as I tell you. And every sensation that I tell you to experience, you will experience exactly as I tell you. From now on, you will experience an absolute distaste of smoking, and all the old feelings you have had of your need to smoke, of your craving to smoke, of your desire to smoke, those old feelings will rapidly and completely diminish. You are now turning away from your smoking addiction, and you are aware of what a positive experience it is to stop smoking. You are beginning to feel very proud of the commitment you made to yourself to stop smoking. No longer are you, or will you ever be again, a slave to that disabling habit. You will now see other people's smoking as a weakness and your not smoking as a strength. You no longer have any desire to inhale the poisonous tars, the poisonous nicotine down into your lungs, turning them black and filling them with mucus. The thought of inhaling a cigarette now in your mind will be like inhaling dirt or mucus, a thought so revolting to you, so disgusting to you that your desire to stay away from cigarettes permanently is so strong, so intense that it completely overwhelms the desire to smoke. The fears of emphysema, of heart disease, of cancer, the shortness of breath, the poor circulation, the loss of energy, these fears, these feelings that every smoker experiences, reinforce your need to stay away from that terribly disabling habit. You continue now to relax, to feel the wonderful, pleasant sensation of relaxation. Just feel the comfort of this relaxation. You have no desire to change it at all. You don't like changing anything, you just want the pleasantness of the relaxation. You need not pursue any other thoughts, just the feeling that you are relaxing deeper, sinking deeper and deeper, away from everything around you. And these feelings of relaxation will bring you greater and greater feelings of comfort, as you feel yourself relaxing down and down, sinking down deeper and deeper as you relax deeper and deeper. Soon you will be able to listen to my voice completely at ease, enjoying the feeling that I described to you. Enjoying the feelings of deep relaxation that are becoming so pleasant to you. While I talk to you, you can just listen, there is nothing for you to do, nothing at all but just listen. Just imagine that all around you, comfortably surrounding you with a soft cushion's relaxation; that this circle of peacefulness allows you just to float and drift and relax, allows you to drift and relax without tension, without stress, without anxiety, without care; just floating, relaxing, doing absolutely nothing at all. And now you will find that you are becoming even more relaxed, just listen to my voice, it relaxes you, it makes you feel as though a pleasant heaviness is slowly spreading through you. Your body relaxing with feelings of pleasant, wonderful heaviness. You feel so comfortable, you're able to listen to me without any effort, without any effort at all. You are drifting further and further away from stress, drifting further from anxiety or from tension; drifting closer and closer to perfect comfort, calmness. You may become so comfortable now, so much at ease the feelings may be so pleasant to you that you may not even have the desire to move. You may only want to rest, to rest deeper and deeper and deeper. And as you rest, once again you think of your purpose of stopping smoking. The image of yourself now with a cigarette is a very ugly one. You will never again choose a cigarette over your own health. You will now choose your health over the cigarette. You will find health far more satisfying than any cigarette could ever be, and you will not replace the smoking habit with any other negative habit, such as overeating. In fact, your appetite will in no way increase, you will have absolutely no craving, no desires for additional food. From now on, you will have the reassuring knowledge that you have stopped doing something detestable to yourself and have done something very positive for yourself. You will have complete and absolute control over the old habit of smoking. There will be absolutely no circumstances in which you would choose to smoke. You realize now that the cigarette offers no escape from tension, no escape from anxiety. You realize now that all the cigarettes have ever done for you is to slowly, sometimes painfully, eat away at your life, at your health like a disease. Just completely relax now; deeper and deeper, and as you relax, as you feel relaxed, all of the feelings, all of the sensations of relaxation that I told you you would feel, you are feeling. And as you relax, as you feel relaxed, all of the feelings, all of the sensations of heaviness that I told you you would feel, you are feeling. Do not resist it, let yourself enjoy it. Relaxation is beneficial to you. You feel at peace, no stress, no strain, no anxiety; and as you relax and as you float, sometimes it may feel that you are drifting away from everything around you. And if you feel this pleasant sensation, don't bother to analyze your thoughts or sensations, just allow your mind to be passive and allow the feelings of quietness to surround you with its protectiveness. Once again, I bring your mind back to stopping smoking. And now you will fully understand that by having stopped smoking, you will completely reverse the cycle of illness and disease, and begin instead the process of cleaning all of the filth, all the damage out of your lungs, out of your body. The process of restoring your health, of repairing the damage and restoring the strength and vitality; this is very relaxing for you to know, that you are going to restore your strength, to repair the damage, restore your health and vitality. So as I now count to you, I count from five to one, and as you let yourself descend down with the numbers, into an even deeper state of relaxation, you will find yourself drifting further and further away from the need of ever needing a cigarette again. Now I am going to begin to count. Five, let yourself drift down, drift further and further away from ever desiring to smoke again. Four, drifting lower. Three, two, one. And all the suggestions I have given you, and all the suggestions I will give you, will be totally effective; and the strength of the suggestions will never waver, will never lessen. They become now a permanent state of mind, continuing every minute of every day. And every day now, without your cigarettes, without smoking, you will become physically and mentally stronger, fitter. Without the cigarettes robbing your energy and dulling your senses, you will become more alert, more wide awake, more energetic. And every day, without the cigarettes constricting your blood vessels, causing your heart to pump harder, you will find that your nerves grow stronger and steadier. For the next few days, you will become so deeply interested in the pride of stopping smoking, so deeply interested in your new feelings of health, that your mind will not be preoccupied with smoking. You will only regard cigarettes with disgust, and even if the thought of a cigarette momentarily occurs to you, you will go right on with whatever you were doing, and the thought will easily pass by, no longer having any effect on you. Every day without the cigarette, your mind will become calmer, clearer, more composed. You will be much less easily worried or agitated. You will be able to think more clearly, concentrate more easily; and from now on you will see the cigarettes in their true perspective, as a filthy, disgusting habit. Never again associating the thought of a cigarette with pleasure, and because you have stopped smoking, every day you will have a greater feeling of personal well-being, a greater feeling of personal safety, a greater feeling of personal security; more than you have felt in a long, long time. And every day without a cigarette, you will become and remain, more and more completely relaxed, both mentally and physically. And as you become, and as you remain more relaxed, less tense, so you will develop much more confidence in yourself; much more confidence in your ability to do whatever you have to do, without the need for a cigarette. And you will have the confidence in your ability to stay away from cigarettes without fear, without anxiety, without tensions, without frustrations, without uneasiness and because of this, every day you will feel more and more independent; independent of the smoking habit, and you will know that no matter how difficult or trying things may be, you will be able to cope with them easily and efficiently without any need for a cigarette at all. Because all these things will happen exactly as I tell you they will happen, you will feel much happier, much more content, much more cheerful, much more optimistic. Remember, there are absolutely no circumstances under which you would ever again choose to smoke. Now you are relaxed, you are able to respond completely to all the suggestions that I have given you, and everything that I told you that you will feel, you *will* feel. And everything that I told is going to happen, *will* happen, exactly as I told you. And every sensation that I told you you would experience, you *will* experience, exactly as I told you. Now in a few moments, I am going to count to seven, and when I reach seven you will open your eyes, you will feel wide awake, and you'll feel wonderfully better for this long and relaxed rest. You will feel completely relaxed, mentally and physically, feeling calm and composed. So gradually now, you can begin to return to a state of normal activity, and as you do, the feelings of heaviness, of limpness, of lethargy will completely and totally disappear. Now, I shall count, and with each number you can become more and more wide awake, calm, composed and wonderfully relaxed. Now, I am going to count. One, two, three, four, five, six, seven. Wake up now. Wake up.

"From now on, whenever you wish to repeat these suggestions at home, all you have to do is to make yourself comfortable and switch on this recording. The moment you hear my voice on the recording, you will immediately begin to respond, and all the suggestions that I give you will take effect just as powerfully each time you hear them. If at any time you are listening, and the recording stops unexpectedly for any reason, or should any emergency occur while you are listening to the recording, then you will open your eyes immediately and be actively aware and fully prepared to take any necessary action."

The Six Changes Required to End Most Habits

If smoking tobacco is not your "cup of tea," you can still use the above tape or monologue for breaking the tea habit. All you have to do is edit it to fit the tea problem.

In fact, the principles behind breaking the cigarette smoking habit work for habits generally. They merely need to be adapted to fit.

Here are six changes that need to take place in you in order to end an unwanted habit:

1. Become aware of the habit.
2. List the reasons why you want to change.
3. Make the decision that you are going to behave in a different way, free of the habit.
4. Set time limits for preparing the tape and beginning your Autogenics modification.
5. Go through the mood setting and the Autogenics tape or monologue to effect the change.
6. Reinforce the change with repetition.

Katherine was a heavy smoker. Her physician examined her lungs and gave her an ultimatum: stop smoking or else. She went to a hypnologist and succeeded, using methods similar to ours. Some time later, she had a stressful emotional experience that caused her to reach for a cigarette. She recognized the danger of becoming addicted again, so she reached for the telephone instead. She called her hypnologist. He was away on a two-week vacation. With a sigh of resignation, she lit up. She went back to cigarettes as before. Soon she was in the hospital with emphysema. She pulled through. This time she came to our office to train herself to be her own hypnologist—and prevented similar relapses.

The above six changes needed to break a habit involve no other person than *you*.

You are in charge. You are in control. You can improve your behavior habits by yourself and keep them improved. You can upgrade your quality of life.

Autogenics for Pot, Alcohol and Drug Addiction

Autogenics to end the habit of smoking marijuana follows the same procedure as smoking tobacco, with one change.

Do not light up as you review the hazards. Your mood-setting review of the hazards of being a pot-head will not "take" while under the influence of pot, any more than it will take for alcohol while drunk or for drugs while "high."

Make a list of the pot-head problems—how they affect your job, your mental ability, your health, your relationships with family, neighbors, colleagues.

Next, edit the monologue, substituting pot for tobacco and revising the programming to fit the new set of hazards.

Alcoholics should do the same for alcohol problems and revising the monologue to conform to alcohol addiction.

Drug users should do the same for drug problems, again revising the monologue to conform to drug addiction.

A word about drug addiction. Do not delay even one day. Autogenics, self-administered will work only in the early stages. Physical addiction later involves physical changes that only professional help can provide and supervise.

David, 37, had a drug abuse problem. It started back in high school. "More recently I started taking drugs everyday because it became my way of thinking. I'm happiest when I'm high."

He came to us because he had no direction, no goal; because he would be faced with repeated psychiatric hospitalizations; because he was tense, depressed, and racked with guilty feelings.

In his initial interview, David narrowed his drug abuse practices to taking "downers" and cough syrup (contains tranquilizers), with occasional resort to harder drugs.

David went through the relaxation and habit control procedures spelled out in these pages. In addition, he used change formulae that lessened his sensitivity to social tensions which occurred mostly at work, and which built up his ego and self-esteem.

A follow-up study in three months found David using his relaxation techniques whenever he felt tense, instead of using drugs. He was able to set goals for himself and had new self-confidence and an improved self-image. In addition, he was attending group sessions at a drug center to lend his support to others.

Note that this was a two-pronged attack just as in the overeating habit. You need to attack the substance. But you may also need to attack the emotional weakness that leads to taking the substance. Refer to the previous chapter for how to do this with Autogenics.

In all of these addiction habits, the mood-setting and the extended relaxation monologue, including change formula statements, should be repeated at first daily and then every few days until there is no more desire for the material.

Autogenics for Habitual Mannerisms and Unwanted Behavior

Non-addictive habits do not need the intensive attack that Autogenics provides for smoking, drinking, etc.

You can succeed with a simple mood formula, a standard relaxation monologue, and a direct change formula.

Assuming you are using your standard relaxation tape or monologue, here are mood and change formulae for common mannerism and behavior habits:

- Nail-biting
- Hair-twisting
- Coffee-drinking
- Thumb-sucking
- Bed-wetting
- Stuttering

Nail-Biting:

Mood formula: See yourself with beautiful nails. You are using your hands in some typical situation, in show off instead of in shame.

Change formula: "My nails are important to me. They are part of the skin of my body. I love and care for them as I do the rest of my body. I have no need to bite my nails.

Whenever I am nervous or tense,
I will take a deep breath and
feel relaxed and confident."

Hair-Twisting:

Mood formula: See yourself in the two-path situation. On the left path, you twiddle and twist your hair. People notice. You are uncomfortable and embarrassed. On the right path, you just stroke your hair once. No one notices. Life is improved. You take the right-hand path.

Change formula: "Twisting the strands of my hair no longer pleases me. It feels irritating. Whenever I feel the desire to feel my hair, I run my hand over my hair once to straighten it and I am fully satisfied."

Coffee-Drinking:

Mood formula: Use the two-path exercise. On the left path you see yourself drinking too much coffee. You see the nervousness, possible effects to your heart. You see brief increases in energy followed by periods of decreased energy—ups and downs. On the right-hand path, you see yourself drinking only one cup in the morning. The rest of the day you are calm and in control. You have steady energy. You are healthier.

Change formula: "My nerves are stronger and steadier. I am able to deal with life as it comes. I have no need for coffee at the end of a meal or in between. I relinquish it."

Thumb-Sucking:

Mood formula: See yourself free of the habit. Your thumb is distasteful to your mouth. See yourself in situations where you are tempted to suck your thumb. You do not. Your hands rest comfortably on your lap.

Change formula: "I dislike the taste of my thumb. I detest its unsanitary condition. Whenever I have the urge to insert my thumb in my mouth, all I need to do is take one deep breath. When I exhale, the urge will be gone."

Bed-Wetting:

Mood formula: See yourself getting up in the middle of the night and going to the bathroom. See what time the clock says. Next see the clock reading the time you usually wake up. Your bed is dry.

Change formula: "I prefer a dry bed to a wet bed. I awake easily when I need to urinate. I go to the bathroom to do it. I return to my bed and fall asleep easily."

Stuttering:

Mood formula: See yourself talking slowly and naturally with no desire to speak any faster and no sign of stuttering. You are confident and relaxed.

Relaxation formula: If you made your relaxation tape with any stuttering in it, use a friend's voice instead.

Change formula: "I no longer pay any attention to my speech. I talk much the same as I walk. As step follows step

> without self-consciousness, so
> word follows word naturally without
> my concern. I am relaxed about
> my speech, more and more relaxed
> with every word I say."

Jeff, 25, was a respiratory therapist. He stuttered practically every time he spoke. It was a professional liability to him. He came to our office because he was angry. "I am fearful at work. I should not feel this way."

With his mood, relaxation, and change steps, Jeff's speech began to improve. Within months he reported feeling more confident, less anxious about his speech, and with less cause for anxiety. He stuttered rarely. He was happy at work and this was being reflected in his skill as a therapist.

Habits can be changed. Hypnotism or self-hypnotism—such as that used in Autogenics—is your best tool.

CHAPTER 9

How to Improve Skills and Abilities

YOU CAN END UNWANTED HABITS. You can also improve on desired habits. Skills and abilities are desirable habits.

The way to improve skills and abilities is to treat them as habits which you want to reinforce.

My co-author, Dr. Robert Stone, has written 68 books in 30 years. Writing is his skill. In 1975 he had written 48 books in 24 years. That is exactly two books a year. Then he used Autogenic methods to improve his skill. In the next six years, he wrote 20 books. That equals three and one-third books a year—an increase of 65 percent!

How did he apply the method? I'll let him tell you.

> "I set the mood every day by picturing myself covering more ground the following day. Then I relaxed. For my change formula, I spent five minutes visualizing. By actual word count, I see my production improving in both quality and quantity from say 1,100 words to 1,200 words. I see new contracts being signed, new books being outlined, and more words being written. I have doubled my daily capability since I started the Autogenics process about six years ago. And my writing is easier and better than ever. Don't take my word for it. Ask my banker."

Instead of asking his banker, why not prove it to yourself? Here is a simple exercise you can do with a rubber ball and a wastepaper basket. Sit in a chair with the basket about ten feet away. If it is too easy to toss the ball into the basket, increase the distance. Now, see how many times you sink the ball out of ten tries. Then close your eyes, relax, and "see" yourself easily sinking every shot. After two or three minutes, open your eyes and throw ten more times. Your score has improved.

Seven Steps That Improve a Skill

The skills which we will cover in this chapter include sports such as tennis, golf, and bowling; physical exercise such as jogging, walking, and swimming; home skills such as sewing, gardening, and typing; as well as writing, bookkeeping, and playing a musical instrument.

As usual, there will be three major steps: The *mood formula,* the *relaxation formula,* and the *change formula.*

I will give you the mood formula and change formula for each of the above skills and abilities. You will use the standard relaxation monologue or tape provided in Chapter 2, starting on page 36. You will add the change formula for the skill you select to the tape before the count-up.

1. You read the mood formula for the skill you wish to develop, as stated below.
2. You sit in a comfortable chair with your cassette player handy, relaxation tape in place (or friend ready to read the Chapter 2 monologue).
3. You mentally review your mood formula.
4. You turn on your cassette (or start your friend reading) and relax.
5. The relaxation (or reading) will move next to the change formula for the skill you are enhancing.
6. The change formula will ask you to spend five minutes visualizing yourself performing your skill perfectly. Do it.
7. At the end of approximately five minutes, count yourself up one to ten feeling wide awake and better than you felt before.

Let's start with sports.

How to Improve Your Bowling, Golf and Tennis

Each mood formula in this chapter will be like daydreaming. You will fantasize.

Daydreaming used to be a dirty word. Having fantasies used to be considered the escape of a "ne'er do well." Not any more.

Imaging, as in daydreaming or fantasizing, is now known to be programming. We are teaching the brain neurons to behave for us in that particular way. Many a daydream used to come true. Now that we know deep relaxation is an integral part of the process, more so-called daydreams are being manifested in people's lives.

You will have an alternative to daydreaming as your mood formula for sports: using the pendulum. I will tell you how later.

Autogenics in Sports

A junior high school boys' basketball squad is divided into two parts. One part practices foul shooting in the gymnasium every afternoon. The other part goes home, relaxes, and imagines they are shooting fouls. Later, each group has improved by the same amount.

A professional baseball team is at the bottom of the league standings. They take a training in relaxed visualization. Within months they move to near the top of the league.

A golf pro plays a practice round on a course before the tournament. Then he goes to his hotel room and relaxes. He imagines he is playing each hole successfully—perfect drive, perfect approach shot, perfect putt. He does this a number of times before the tournament begins. He wins.

The muscles of the body respond to mental pictures. You demonstrated this earlier with the shopping bag and the balloon. This is what causes many physical problems and what enables us to correct them, too.

An Australian actor, F. Matthias Alexander, back in 1894 was stricken with voice loss. Realizing that his mind caused this, he devised a mental exercise that quickly corrected it. Today, the Alexander Technique is taught by hundreds of specialists around the world. Its basic approach is to think in a certain way as you change positions or move. You think, "Let my neck be free to let my head go forward and up to permit my back to lengthen and widen." By picturing this happening, the body straightens, posture improves, internal tensions and imbalances are corrected, and physical problems disappear.

The physical problem that disappears in basketball—missing the basket—does so because instead of fear of failure you substitute mental images of the perfect shot. The same happens in golf, in baseball, and in any physical sport where improvement is sought.

Autogenics for Tennis Players, Golfers and Bowlers

I am going to assume that all readers know what a developed skill looks like in their respective sports, skills, or abilities.

If you have never seen a good tennis game, a professional golfer on the course, or top bowlers in action, do not read further. You must seek out the opportunity to view top talent at work. This is true even if you want to improve your gardening or sewing—no matter what the skill or ability.

This is because the key is visualizing yourself performing at a "top talent" level. You must know what that looks like.

If you have this picture, you are ready to begin. We will cover skill sports first. We will cover tennis, golf, and bowling. But you will see how to adapt the wording for any other skill sport, such as basketball, football, baseball, Ping Pong, billiards, etc.

First step: Add to your relaxation tape the change formula below. Where several choices are given, the first line is for bowlers, the second for golfers, and the third is for tennis players.

Once the tape is made, you are ready to begin. Use the mood formula. Turn on the relaxation tape which ends with the change formula. Spend five minutes visualizing yourself as the perfect player. Count yourself up feeling wide awake, using the basic procedure under "Coming Out."

Mood Formula. What benefits will accrue to you as a better (bowler) (golfer) (tennis) player? See these benefits taking place—acclamation, more money, more fun, more recognition, more satisfaction, etc. Spend a minute or two doing this.

Change Formula. Because now you are relaxed, your subconscious mind is concentrating its attention on what I am saying and each suggestion I will give you will sink deeper and deeper into the subconscious part of your mind, and the suggestions I give you will benefit you. The suggestions will take hold easily and quickly and your mind will, from now on, use the suggestions automatically whenever you need them, because from now on your confidence in your ability to (bowl) (play golf) (play tennis) will become greater and greater. You will have the ability to build and maintain your confidence. Your self-confidence will not be affected by minor events or mistakes. Other people will not be able to negatively affect your confidence or to lessen it in any way. Your feelings of confidence will not be restricted to (bowling) (golf) (tennis), but will be directed at everything that you do. Also, your powers of concentration will increase. You will be able to totally observe the game, and purely through your keen observation (at the bowling lanes) (on the golf course) (on the tennis court), you will be able to totally focus your attention on each movement of the game; each of your movements and each of your opponent's movements. You will trust your mind completely and you will know that, by observing, your mind will concentrate and accurately control your every play. Your mind will not wander, it will totally observe and make accurate decisions and judgments. You will now be able to practice and correct your (bowling) (golf game) (tennis game) mentally by visualizing yourself making each movement, each shot exactly the way it should be played. You will be able to visualize yourself (making strikes, getting spares) (driving, using irons, putting) (serving, your forehand, your backhand), and each (movement) of your game. You can practice this visualization in slow motion and then gradually increase the speed of your visualization until you see yourself at normal speed. Remember, once you program the correct movements into your subconscious, your mind will do the rest for you when you are actually playing. Your subconscious will program your thoughts and your moves exactly as you program them to do. In a few moments, I am going to stop talking. At that point, you can do your mental visualization. Repeat it until you are comfortable with it. You now have five minutes for a visualization practice, starting from now. (Five-minutes time lapse.)

Coming Out. In a moment, I will count to five. At five, I will open my eyes; I will feel wonderful, positive and assertive concerning myself and my (bowling) (golf) (tennis) game. Now I am going to count from one to five. When I reach number five, I will open my eyes feeling wide awake, fully alert, both mentally and physically, just as if I were waking up from a long, restful nap. When I open my eyes, I am going to feel wonderful, both physically and mentally. I am going to feel better than I have felt in a long, long time, and when I open my eyes, I will know and realize that all of the ideas and suggestions that I received are now part of me, and will stay with me indefinitely, growing stronger and stronger as each day goes by. Now I am going to count. One, two, drifting higher and higher toward normal wakefulness, three, what a wonderful feeling, four, higher and higher, five. I open my eyes, feeling wonderfully refreshed.

How to Use the Pendulum as an Aid in Sports

In 1812, a French physician and scientist named Chevreul recognized the influence of the mind over the body functions.

To prove his point, he demonstrated the effect with the aid of a pendulum—the kind we created with a button on a string.

He would ask his patient to hold the chain so that the point of the weighted end was suspended about one inch over the center of a small circle. He then asked the subject to concentrate strongly on the pendulum and to force it, by his mind's power alone, to begin to sway. The direction is not important. Soon the pendulum, now controlled by the subject's mind, would begin to sway.

Chevreul next instructed the subject to concentrate on a specific direction, for example a clockwise, circular motion. Soon the pendulum would begin to change direction and move in the direction of a small circle. Very soon, with practice, the subject could cause the pendulum to move in any direction that he "willed" it to.

This phenomenon has become a standard in the exercise of concentration. You can use it to improve your tennis game. When you apply this principle to your game, it will produce a super-ability of concentration and accuracy for you, causing the tennis ball to land in any specific spot determined by *your* mind. Here is how.

Step #1. Practice with the pendulum until you can cause the pendulum to move in any direction you choose, by pure mind power alone. Do not attempt to influence the movement of the pendulum by consciously moving your fingers or your hand. Simply hold the chain between your thumb and your index finger.

Step #2. On the tennis court, utilize the same principle to concentrate on where you want the ball to land, without exercising specific changes in the manner in which you hold your tennis racket. As you stroke, use your mind power. With persistent practice, your accuracy wil increase by leaps and bounds.

Autogenics to Help with Walking, Jogging and Swimming

There is more attention to exercise these days than perhaps ever in recent American history. The reason is health. Research shows that walking and jogging not only help to stave off circulatory diseases, but also help to relieve them.

You can use Autogenics to gradually improve your stamina as well as to perfect your style so as to enhance the beneficial effects of walking, jogging, running and swimming.

Again, experience the mood formula below; play the relaxation tape which you have extended with the change formula below; take five minutes to visualize yourself moving rhythmically and with perfect ease and form; and end your session with the "Coming Out" procedure given under tennis above, of course substituting your activity for the word "tennis."

Mood Formula. What improvements in your looks, health, and energy do you expect as a result of your physical work-out?

Change Formula. Because now you are relaxed, your subconscious mind is concentrating its attention on what I am saying and each suggestion I give you will sink deeper and deeper into the subconscious part of your mind, and the suggestions I give you will benefit you. The suggestions will take hold easily and quickly and your mind will, from now on, use the suggestions automatically whenever you need them, because from now on your confidence in your ability to (swim) (jog) (walk) for health will become greater and greater. You will know the speed and distance that are right for you at the time. You will have the ability to build and maintain both your stamina and your confidence. Your self-confidence will not be affected by minor events or non-valid self-limiting ideas. Other people will not be able to negatively affect your confidence or to lessen your stamina in any way. Your feelings of confidence will not be restricted to (swimming) (jogging) (walking) but will be directed at everything you do. Also, your powers of concentration will increase. You will be able to totally observe your activity and purely through your keen observation of your movements, you will be able to relax overly tense muscles to make your movements more natural and more rhythmic. You will trust your mind completely and you will know that, by observing, your mind will concentrate and accurately control your motion all the way. Your mind will not wander, it will totally observe and make accurate decisions and judgments. You will now be able to practice (swimming) (jogging) (walking) mentally by visualizing yourself making each movement, exactly the way it should be made. You will be able to visualize yourself beginning your (swim) (jog) (walk), entering into it with vigor but without wasted effort, making each movement naturally and in perfect form. You can practice this visualization in slow motion and then gradually increase the speed of your visualization until you see yourself at normal speed. Remember, once you program the correct movements into your subconscious, your mind will do the rest for your when you are actually (swimming) (jogging) (walking). Your subconscious will program your thoughts and your moves exactly as you program them to do. In a few moments, I am going to stop talking. At that point, you can do your mental visualization. Repeat it until you are comfortable with it. You now have five minutes for a visualization practice, starting from now. (Five-minute time lapse then come out as with tennis.)

Autogenics to Improve Your Typing, Sewing, or Musical Skill

Some skills are learned. Others come naturally. Both types can be improved with practice. Both can be improved faster with Autogenics.

Let us examine three typical skills that are usually learned. Most people learn how to type in school. The same goes for serious sewing and also playing a musical instrument. We will now give the mood formula and change formula for each of these.

If you happen to be one of the exceptions where either typing, sewing, or playing the piano has come naturally or is self-taught, the procedure is no different.

Everyone can improve a learned skill if he knows what that improvement means. Just as we discussed how a tennis player must have seen expert players on the court before he can expect to move his own expertise in that direction, so it is with the typist; the knitter, sewer, crocheter or embroiderer; the guitarist, the pianist, or the violinist. You must know what "good" is.

Some of the other skills or abilities that respond to the procedures in this section include gourmet cooking, home improvements and repairs, hobbies and handcrafts. You need to adapt the mood formula to enhance the feeling of reward that comes with that activity. You need to adapt the change formula to reflect the upgrading of the separate skill components that comprise that activity.

Once again, the tape or monologue you use for relaxation must be extended with the change formula below. Then you are ready to set the mood, relax, accept the change formula, "daydream" five minutes, and count yourself up.

OM

Mood Formula—*Typing*. See yourself typing letters, papers, reports, manuscripts—everything that you usually type or would type if your typing was better. Feel the pride of having produced a professionally typed product. See yourself typing easily, rapidly, correctly, and with no need to eye the keys. Feel the joy of being a skilled typist.

oh

Mood Formula—*Sewing*. See yourself as a skilled sewer, embroiderer, crocheter, or knitter—whichever skill you wish to enhance. Feel the pride of having produced a product of value that attracts admiration. Imagine how you will feel being able to accomplish anything in this line that you decide to do, easily, quickly, and skillfully.

Mood Formula—*Playing a Musical Instrument.* See yourself playing socially or professionally. Others are listening, then applauding. You play with talent and feeling. You have a large repertoire of musical pieces. You keep learning new ones easily and well. You are a master of the instrument.

Change Formula. Because now you are relaxed, your subconscious mind is concentrating its attention on what I am saying and each suggestion I will give you will sink deeper and deeper into the subconscious part of your mind, and the suggestions I give will benefit you. The suggestions will take hold easily and quickly and your mind will, from now on, use the suggestions automatically whenever you need them, because from now on your confidence in your ability to (play the ________) (sew) (type) will become greater and greater. You will have the ability to build and maintain your confidence. Your self-confidence will not be affected by minor events or mistakes. Other people will not be able to negatively affect your confidence or to lessen it in any way. Your feelings of confidence will not be restricted to (playing the ________) (sewing) (typing) but will be directed at everything that you do. Also, your powers of concentration will increase.

(Typing will become second nature to you. You will be able to observe the material to be typed while your mind controls your fingers accurately on the keyboard. Your mind will not wander. You will trust your mind completely. Your speed will improve. Your accuracy will continue.)

(Sewing will become second nature to you. Your speed will improve. You will be able to make more-even stitches, know the right amount of thread for a hand repair project, judge measurements visually with accuracy, sew neatly with a professional look, cut correctly, follow patterns correctly, sew straighter with a machine.)

Special Note: Knitters, crocheters and embroiderers should substitute their own change formula phrases for the sewing phrases describing the skill ingredients that apply.

(Playing the ________ will become second nature to you. You will be able to control your (breath) (fingers) effortlessly and precisely. Your motions will reflect the inner nature of the music. Your talent will increase. New pieces will become familiar to you quickly. Your mind will not wander. You will trust your mind completely. You will move closer and closer to being a musical genius.)

You will now be able to practice and correct your skill mentally by visualizing yourself making each movement exactly the way it should be done. You can practice this visualization in slow motion and then gradually increase the speed of your visualization until you see yourself at normal speed. Remember, once you program the correct movements into your subconscious, your mind will do the rest for you when you are actually (playing the ________) (sewing) (typing). Your subconscious will program your thoughts and your moves exactly as you program them to do. In a few moments, I am going to stop talking. At that point, you can do your mental visualization. Repeat it until you are comfortable with it. You now have five minutes for a visualization practice, starting from now. (Five-minutes time lapse.)

Autogenics for Successful Gardening, Bookkeeping and Writing

This final section is devoted to non-related skills and abilities so you can better understand the application of Autogenics to improve any skill or ability that will make you more money, more efficient, or provide more enjoyment.

We all yearn to be good at what we do. But yearning is only the start. It helps to set the mood. Then it takes experiencing by watching and doing. Most people stop there, if they get to this stage in the first place. But in Autogenics, we know improvement then comes through practice, and much faster through visualized practice.

Again, it will be necessary to add to your relaxation tape or monologue using the applicable change formula below. Again, you will go through the mood formula, the relaxation with change formula, your five minutes of visualized practice and your session-ending count-up.

Mood Formula—*Gardening*. See yourself surrounded by the growing things you seek—such as house plants; or a vegetable, flower, or herb garden; or neatly cut lawns and trimmed hedges. Make the picture real. See the colors. Smell the fragrances. Hear the admiration you receive from others.

Mood Formula—*Bookkeeping.* See yourself making the daily entries and enjoying it. See the balanced statements and the monthly or annual reports or tax returns. See the benefits of a job well done. OM

Mood Formula—*Writing.* See yourself writing letters, articles, or books in an interesting, creative manner. See the readers getting your well-communicated messages. If you write to sell, see acceptance letters, contracts, advances, royalties. See them grow in amounts. See good reviews. Feel the pride of authorship. OM

Change Formula. Because now you are relaxed, your subconscious mind is concentrating its attention on what I am saying and each suggestion I will give you will sink deeper and deeper into the subconscious part of your mind, and the suggestions I will give will benefit you. The suggestions will take hold easily and quickly and your mind will, from now on, use the suggestions automatically whenever you need them, because from now on your confidence in your ability to (write) (do bookkeeping) (garden) will become greater and greater. You will have the ability to build and maintain your confidence. Your self-confidence will not be affected by minor events or mistakes. Other people will not be able to negatively affect your confidence or to lessen it in any way. Your feelings of confidence will not be restricted to (writing) (bookkeeping) (gardening) but will be directed at everything that you do. Also, your powers of concentration will increase. OC

(Gardening will come naturally to me. If I need special information, I will know where to find it. I will understand the needs of each plant, its soil requirements and other environmental needs. By filling these needs, I will maintain plants, whether for beauty or for food, at a high level of hardiness and resistance to pests. My ability to prune, to weed, and to plant will improve. My physical prowess will improve as I stoop, bend and kneel with the least stress to my body. My enjoyment will intensify as I find myself more and more in tune with nature.)

(Bookkeeping will come naturally to me. Credits and debits fit into place. I work bookkeeping machines deftly and accurately or, if necessary, I add mentally with speed and accuracy. I understand reconciliation of bank statements, making and balancing daily entries into journals and ledgers. I work easily with payroll matters and other bookkeeping activities. Numbers appeal to me.)

(Writing will come more and more naturally to me. My vocabulary increases. The right words come to me at the right time. I am able to organize my thoughts and put them into succinct phrases. Where indicated, I can be poetic, creative, and imaginative. I can write better and better for longer and longer periods. My writing production improves every time I write.)

You will now be able to practice and improve your (writing) (bookkeeping) (gardening) mentally by visualizing yourself doing it exactly the way it should be done. You can practice this visualization in slow motion and then gradually increase the speed of your visualization until you see yourself at normal speed. Remember, once you program the correct movements into your subconscious, your mind will do the rest for you when you are actually playing. Your subconscious will program your thoughts and your moves exactly as you program them to do. In a few moments, I am going to stop talking. At that point, you can do your mental visualization. Repeat it until you are comfortable with it. You now have five minutes for a visualization practice, starting from now. (Five-minute time lapse.)

End your session after approximately five minutes of "mental practice." Use your count-up, giving yourself instructions to "feel wide awake and better than I felt before."

CHAPTER 10

Autogenics for Solving Daily Problems

HAVE YOU EVER HAD AN I.Q. TEST? Intelligence Quotient is the term given to the level you attain on a test designed to measure your mental ability.

Usually a quotient of 100 indicates you are average in your age bracket. A score of 150 would mean you are way ahead of your peers, in fact near a genius level.

Even at an I.Q. of 150, you would be using only a fraction of your brain.

From the moment of conception to the moment of birth, the brain is developing at the rate of 4,000 neurons a second. Most of them need not have bothered. It has been estimated that 80 percent may be largely unused in a lifetime.

If we can program our brain to behave in a different way or in a more skillful manner, is it possible to program our brain for more of the neurons to get into the act?

The answer is an emphatic *yes*!

One well-known British researcher was so dead set against this idea that he "fixed" the results of his experiments in order to prove that we are born smart or stupid. This cost mankind a few decades of progress in this area. When other scientists got different results, the original work was re-examined and the fraud uncovered.

Today, a number of disciplines involving relaxed programming teach students how to activate more of their minds to go to work for them in order to cope better with not only the daily problems that most people have, but also those "Catch 22" problems where no acceptable solution appears to exist.

In this chapter we will apply Autogenics to the more common daily problems. In the next chapter we will hit the tougher ones.

I have good news for those of you who have been putting the book down and using Autogenics. If you have experienced the relaxation tape or monologue at least five times, you are now ready to relax on your own. You have programmed yourself to relax and will now remember enough of the process to be successful at it.

Of course, you may still play the tape if you wish, or you may use the services of the person who has been good enough to read the monologue to you. But you are now an experienced relaxer and able to take matters into your own mental and physical control.

I encourage this. After all, when you learn to use Autogenics to help your health, your personality, your habits, your skills, and your success, you are learning to take charge of your life.

The moment you switch from tape or monologue to your own procedure, you take a decisive step forward in control. This in turn leads to a more positive and assured self-concept which in turn permits more of your brain—up until now held back by a more limited self-concept—to go to work for you in bringing about solutions to daily problems.

Harriet programmed herself so that the wailing of the infant next door would no longer get on her nerves but would relax her more and more. Result: Instead of being "bugged" by the crying and forced to stop what she was doing, she hardly noticed it any more.

Steven was being hurt by his constantly increasing electric bill. He and his wife turned out lights where possible but rates kept going up due to fuel costs. More cuts had to be made. But where? He did a mood formula, went to his relaxed state, and instructed his mind to make him aware of ways to cut electric use. Result: He found more efficient use of range burners, turned off the hot water heater at night, and found a score of ways to save electricity by 20 percent.

Edwina and her husband were outgrowing their home. It was not so much a question of bedrooms as of storage space. Their possessions were increasing and closets were starting to bulge. Edwina was forced to use Autogenics instead of a building contractor because of rising costs and interest rates. Result: She became aware of more efficient ways to store in existing places and of more places to store that could be developed with hardly any expense.

This is one habit most of us have. We hear of somebody using a technique successfully and we say, "Well, that was OK for him, but in my case..."

The noise you just heard was that habit breaking.

This chapter is "your case."

Preparing to Focus on Your Own Special Targets

Sometimes special individual problems require special individual approaches. We are going to provide these approaches—enough of them so that you can design your own approach for just about any kind of problem that arises in your case.

But, more often than not, special individual problems require standard general approaches. These approaches have already been supplied, especially in Chapters 3, 4, 5, and 6. These focus on negativity, and feelings of inadequacy. They reprogram you from such limiting feelings to the more positive, self-assured feelings that automatically trigger more of your brain to go to work for you.

Nobody likes to take the blame for problems or failure to solve them. But just as we cause our own lack of resistance to disease, we also cause our own family, work and social problems. We do this certainly to the extent that we block solutions. And when we feel we are unable to solve a particular problem, we are in effect ordering our brain to continue to function at only a fraction of its ability, thus blocking its ability to deliver a solution.

No matter what problems are prevalent in your case, the best way to start is to use Autogenics to improve your own opinion of yourself. Refer to the following pages as a refresher:

Here are some positive suggestions to use for change formulae:

I am relaxed, calm and composed in any situation.
I have absolute and complete control of my emotions.
I am able to dissolve tension before it builds.
I am patient, understanding, and compassionate.

I get along easily with others.
I am capable and efficient.
I have genius-like mental abilities.

These qualities may be unlike you at the present. But after several Autogenics sessions, the above words will describe you accurately.

You may then find that the particular problems for which you are reading this chapter will have disappeared. This often happens as we change in the direction of having a more relaxed demeanor plus a better opinion of ourselves.

If the problem or problems still exist, their days are numbered. The power of your mind will be focused on them. That power, when focused, is like a laser beam—able to dissolve and to recreate.

The focusing procedure will now require a simple device. On a piece of standard typing paper, create a black circle about three inches in diameter. You can use india ink or a black felt pen or any other drawing or writing instrument that will enable you to create this solid black circle. It should be placed at the center of the page.

You will be using this "target" to aid your Autogenics concentration. Here is how.

Selecting Stocks or Bonds, or Making Other Multiple-Choice Decisions

Jerry, a young stock broker, came to me with quite an interesting problem. His job was to seek out information on various companies and to recommend purchases of stock based upon his research. His batting average was miserable, he admitted, but he said in anger, "If I would have made my first choice, I would have been right most of the time."

I asked him to describe this to me in greater detail and he explained, "I get an impulse about a certain stock, but I don't trust my first impulses so I evaluate further and further and eventually convince myself about another stock. And in most cases, unfortunately, I am wrong."

We talked for a while about Jerry's background. He had been interested in stocks since he was 13 years old and at 16 was a regular reader of *The Wall Street Journal* and a number of other stock reports. Then he got an M.A. and a B.S.C. in Science and Business Administration and now worked for a large national brokerage firm.

I asked him whether his original impulse to buy stock was just intuition or based upon knowledge. He didn't seem to know, but he believed it was mainly based upon knowledge. I asked him why he did not attempt to select the stock based upon his first impulse and his response to me was, "Well that's the way to go down the tube."

"But," I argued, "you have a record here that shows that if you would have purchased the stock based upon your original impulse you would have done very well."

His response to that was, "Yes, pure luck."

"Do you believe that all the knowledge that you have is presently in your mind and that if you could present a problem to your mind, the knowledge within your mind could solve the problem?" I asked.

He replied affirmatively.

The direction that we then took was that he feed into his mind the potential stocks that he would be likely to recommend; then allow his mind to decide upon the stock that should be purchased. He would read what he could and learn what he could about each particular stock, allow his mind to digest the information, and then respond with the stock that he should purchase.

The system worked well. He began to grow more and more confident in his ability to choose stocks. Recently, he has begun to issue his own newsletter which has been well received. One day he reminded me that the system I had introduced might have been borrowed from a story he read about the late millionnaire financier Bernard Baruch, who claimed that his success was based upon reading all he could read about a company, then going to bed and posing the problem to himself—which of these stocks should I purchase? Mr. Baruch claimed that the next morning he woke up with a name on his mind, wrote it down, and went out to purchase the stock.

My only response to Jerry was, "Well, if it was good enough for Mr. Baruch..."

And it should be good enough for you, too. Mr. Baruch had no more brain neurons than Jerry, and no more brain neurons than you. All Jerry and Mr. Baruch did was to order their brain neurons to get to work on the problem.

Most of our brain neurons are loafing. We have ordered them to loaf. ("I am a B student." "I am not as smart as so-and-so." "I am only a $15,000-a year person.") Now, we are going to order more of our brain neurons to get into the ball game.

You are going to use two devices to help you make the right decision on life's multiple-choice problems: The target you just prepared according to the above instructions; and the button on a string that you prepared and used according to the instructions on page 60. You will not be using the button on a string as a pendulum the way you did before. Instead, you will be using it as a triggering device. You will program your brain to work better for you on multiple-choice problems merely by touching it.

Here are some typical multiple-choice questions in business:

- Selecting the right stocks, bonds, or other investments.
- Buying, selling, waiting, selling short.
- Selecting one of several possible locations, products, or brokers.
- Employing a key person from several available candidates.
- Assigning a project to the right employee.

Here are some typical multiple-choice questions in private life:

- Selecting the right movie or show to see.
- Choosing the right person for you.
- Deciding on a vacation spot.
- Picking a job when more than one is offered.
- Selecting the vitamins your body needs.

Here is the procedure to follow to apply Autogenics to help in the solution.

1. Learn all you can about each of the alternatives available to you. Read, ask questions, seek out information from all possible dependable sources.

2. Hang your target circle on the wall five to ten feet from the chair you will use, in a position that will allow you to look at it comfortably while relaxing.

3. Relax and set the mood by concentrating on the black dot of your target. Keep your eyes on this "bull's eye." Close your eyes, and where the target was, see action being taken as if the answer was already known, i.e., you are buying or selling a stock or your are on your way to the movie of your choice.

4. Relax as if you were playing your tape or listening to the spoken monologue. Be comfortable about relaxing on your own. Repeat the countdown or feeling of sleepiness or other parts of the relaxation procedures with which you are familiar, if you desire further deepening.

5. Give yourself the following instructions as your change formula:

> *"I have a problem (identify it to yourself mentally). I have all of the information I need to select the best solution. It will be provided by my Intelligence Filter asleep in a dream or awake as a flash of insight, within the next 24 hours. Every time I finger this pendulum* (hold button between thumb and forefinger) *I reinforce this instruction. My awareness intensifies and I function at a higher level of wisdom and intelligence."*

6. Pause before ending your session. Open your eyes slightly, just enough to see the target circle again. Close them and invite a solution to come into your perception. If none comes, repeat:

> *"I have all of the information I need to select the best solution to the problem. The solution will come to me asleep or awake within the next 24 hours."*

(Release the pendulum.)

7. End your Autogenics session by counting yourself up and giving yourself instructions that you will feel wide awake when you reach the end of your count, at a high level of well-being. Carry your pendulum with you to finger at will.

How to Obtain Solutions to Chronic Money Problems

There are many prosperity and success seminars held in the major cities of the United States. To varying degrees, they are themselves prospering and successful. If they can be said to have a common denominator, it is "Think positively."

It is pretty hard to think positively when your checks have just bounced, the payment on the car is due, and a pile of unpaid bills is monopolizing your desk.

Yet, a change of polarity in your thinking is essential if a change of polarity in your bank account from minus to plus is to take place. Autogenics supplies the breakthrough.

The mood formula is the key. You can set a positive mood by daydreaming about yourself with all the money you need.

"Hold it," you say. "I've done that many times and where has it got me?"

"Cool it," I reply. "You have probably not been daydreaming in exactly that way."

Most people daydream not about a better house, but about a dream home; not about the bills being all paid up, but about having a million dollars; not about taking the next step up the job ladder, but about being at the top.

Remember, I said "all the money you need," not "all the money you want."

A change in polarity need only go from minus to plus one. The rest will follow, step by step.

Let's look at your financial picture, dividing it up into the income and outgo pictures, that is the cash flow; and then into the balance sheet picture, that is, assets and liabilities.

There will be an improvement in your financial picture cash-flow-wise if any one or more of these types of things occur:

- You discontinue certain cost activities.
- You cut down on other cost activities.
- You find ways to continue activities at a lesser cost.
- You consolidate your debts with a long-term, reasonable interest loan.
- You increase your income by getting a pay raise.
- You increase your income by investing savings at a better interest rate.
- You increase your income by increasing your production.
- You borrow on your life insurance and invest the money at a higher interest than you pay.
- You increase your income by working overtime.

- You increase your income by turning equity into savings at interest (becoming a renter instead of owner).
- You increase your income by adding another source of income (job, hobby, boarder, etc.)
- You buy and sell something at a profit (antiques, securities, etc.).

There will be an improvement in your financial picture, balance-sheet-wise, if one or more of these types of things occur:

- You increase the value of your car or home by maintenance or improvements.
- You sell some unneeded possessions at a profit (paintings, jewelry, antiques, etc.)
- You receive a gift or money from some unexpected source (refund, bequest, etc.).
- A debt is reduced or forgiven.
- An investment or security or possession goes up in value.
- You find something of value you did not know you had.

These are not the only ways that your financial picture can improve. They are merely examples of the many ways in which the problem can be solved.

The first step is to make your brain less problem-oriented and more solution-oriented. Here is how.

1. Study the above alternatives one at a time. Ponder how they might apply to your situation. Think of other alternatives. Make a list of those you might act on.

2. Ready your target circle on the wall as explained earlier in this chapter.

3. Relax and do your mood formula by concentrating on the bull's eye with your eyes open, then closing your eyes and seeing yourself living as you are now but with a surplus of money coming in, enough to pay your expenses and have some leftovers for vacations and savings and whatever else you need to do.

4. Relax with or without your tape or monologue, remembering the feeling of relaxation and inducing it with progressive muscle relaxation, countdowns, peaceful scenes, or feelings of heaviness or drowsiness, etc. Be blissfully relaxed and then deepen it even further.

5. Give yourself the following instructions as your change formula:

> *"I make the decision against money problems and in favor of money solutions. Money can now come to me at a faster rate. My wealth can now increase. I have all the intelligence, the information, the skills, to make this happen starting now. My Intelligence Filter will provide me with ideas. I will act on them. Every time I finger this pendulum* (hold button between thumb and forefinger) *it will trigger my Intelligence Filter to provide money solutions, and my actions."*

6. End your Autogenics session by counting yourself up, giving yourself instructions that you will feel wide awake, great when you open your eyes.

Carry your pendulum with you. Finger it from time to time.

How to Reverse Mental Lethargy, Feelings of Failure and Motivational Lack

Lillian had to compete with three men for the position of executive vice-president. She had been with the plastics company for over 15 years. She was responsible, conscientious, motivated and energetic.

However, for the past six months—as the opportunity to become executive vice-president neared—she became less conscientious, less motivated and less energetic. She was becoming almost irresponsible and had a "couldn't care less" attitude. She attributed this to a feeling of failure regarding her future. After all, what chance did a woman have against three men.

It was not until the date was set for her interview with the company president that she came to life. She made an appointment with me to discuss her negativity and what could be done about it. By now you know what I "prescribed."

There had never been a woman in the executive office before and Lillian believed that if she had the confidence to carry it off, she would really be the best qualified for the position. During the therapy she saw herself clearly, entering the president's office. She saw herself confident, knowledgeable and self-assured. After just one session, she was convinced that she could carry this interview off. She was taught how to reinforce this image by going through the same procedures at home.

Soon it became time for her interview. She was the one selected. Today, she is a successful executive vice-president. But now she has changed her visualizations slightly. Now she visualizes herself sitting in the president's office, displaying confidence, self-assurance and knowledge.

If you were in Lillian's shoes, you would set the mood by looking into your hand mirror and addressing yourself as "Madame Vice-President." You would then relax with or without the tape or monologue. Finally, you would give yourself a confidence-building change formula, including the pendulum-touching as an "instant" reinforcement.

If you are not your energetic self... If you are intimidated by some challenge that lies ahead... If you are despondent about your chances to succeed... If you lack motivation to do what you know needs doing... Then you are indeed in Lillian's shoes, and here is the Autogenics procedure to follow:

1. Set the mood by looking into your hand mirror and seeing yourself over the hump. You have responded to the challenge. You have succeeded. You look relieved and proud. You feel the satisfaction of success. You have confidence in yourself—in your capability, your knowledge, and your intelligence.

2. Relax deeply. Use the hand levitation of the Chapter 3 monologue as part of your deepening technique. Have the pendulum handy, ready to finger.

3. When blissfully relaxed, begin your change formula by seeing yourself increasing in activity—doing what needs to be done. Notice how business-like, efficient, professional and capable you are. Put it into words and repeat them to yourself.

> "*I am energetic. I do what needs to be done. I am confident, intelligent, knowledgeable, and efficient. I am successful.*" End by fingering the pendulum and affirming, "*Every time I finger this pendulum in this way, my Intelligence Filter is triggered to provide me with all I need to know to carry out my objectives, my*

Autogenic session is reinforced and I experience greater awareness, confidence and effectiveness.''

4. End your session with the usual ''feeling great'' count-up.

Coping with Daily People Problems

Daily problems do not always originate within us. A pesky neighbor, an irritable supervisor, a wandering spouse—these are common problems with which we are faced.

Autogenics can help here, too. How can your Autogenics affect another person? The answer lies in an understanding of how we all affect one another all the time.

Experiments conducted at a Brooklyn hospital several decades ago showed that a person could affect another person's dreams. When the subject was asleep, the second person concentrated on a photograph; for example—Santa Claus. When biofeedback equipment indicated the sleeper was dreaming, the sleeper was awakened. ''Funny. I was just dreaming about Christmas.''

We affect each other awake and asleep, consciously and subconsciously.

In Autogenics we change the affect we have on another person from problem reinforcing to solution reinforcing. What happens can appear miraculous to us. But it is a simple cause-effect event. By causing a change in our own attitude, we affect the person differently. As a result:

- A pesky neighbor becomes more cooperative.
- A member of the opposite sex is attracted to you more.
- A spouse is more attentive.
- A supervisor is more amicable.
- A co-worker is more considerate.
- A customer is more likely to buy.
- A child is more reasonable.

You know the process now. But you are probably not convinced that taking unilaterial action through Autogenics is going to affect another person. That is my problem with you.

If I use my Autogenics right now, before writing further, and then continue to write, the problem I have with you is going to disappear. Will that convince you that another person can be affected? All right, then. Here goes...

I have just completed an Autogenics session. My Mood Formula was reviewing in my mind the thousands of letters I have received. Girl meets boy. Boy meets girl. Enemies make amends. Handshakes. Tears. Hugs. Lives are changed.

I relaxed quickly. I have trained myself over the years to be able to relax instantly. Then I used as my Change Formula, pictures of me writing just the right words to encourage you to believe that Autogenics can help you solve a problem with another person. I saw you responding. I felt a closeness to you, despite distance and time. I ended my session.

Feel something? Do we affect one another? Now is it worth a try? Here are the quick and easy steps:

1. *Mood Formula:* Get comfortable. Daydream about one or two persons in the same category (neighbors, supervisors, opposite sex, etc.) with whom you have had a good relationship in the past.
2. *Relaxation Formula:* Dealer's choice. Select any familiar procedures used earlier.
3. *Change formula:* "I forgive *(insert name of problem person)* and I ask forgiveness." See person responding warmly. "I will reflect (sexuality) (friendliness) (cooperation) (*select appropriate word*) with this person at all times. My Intelligence Filter will provide me with understanding, and with the right words and actions so that I will always radiate a loving and positive energy to ______.
4. End session, feeling good about ______.

CHAPTER 11

Coping with Impossible Situations And Insoluble Problems

IN THIS CHAPTER, we extend your abilities for problem-solving and for affecting other people. In the last chapter you crawled. In this chapter you walk, trot, and run.

You gain irresistible energy.

You become a super-learner and super-charged idea generator.

You expand time so there is enough of it to complete your increased activities.

You gain control over others to move toward goals.

You win support for your ideas and projects.

If you have been merely scanning this book, are now attracted by the title of this chapter and its opening remarks, and decide "This one is for me," forget it. This one is not for beginners. You need to go back and do what is asked of you in the first three chapters, and practice what is provided in at least two or three of the subsequent chapters, including Chapter 10 which is a prerequisite to this chapter. You have to crawl before you walk.

Let me remind you of something you already know. Within your mind there is a section that we have called the Intelligence Filter. When you have contacted the Intelligence Filter and posed the problem to it, the Intelligence Filter interprets the problem, finds a pathway to the solution, and accomplishes that goal.

The Intelligence Filter is a super-genius. Yours is. Mine is. Everyone's is. It has at its disposal incredible resources. It can accomplish what you have been unable to conceive as possible. It works in a calm, logical and precise manner to take you through all the necessary steps in orderly sequence to arrive at your desired goal.

All you have to do is give the problem to your Intelligence Filter and then get out of its way.

We do get in our own way. When we relax, we take the first step to getting out of our own way. When we create a solution mood to replace a worrisome problem mood, we step further out of our own way. When we image ourselves in a confident, creative way, we complete the process of getting out of our own way.

If we had not got into our own way to in the first place, we would not have had to resort to Autogenics in the second place, as there would have been no problem to begin with. The Intelligence Filter would have been able to find the answer and take us there without so much as a pause. Now it will do so with a pause—long enough for you to go through the Mood Formula, Relaxation Formula, and Change Formula.

Life offers a steady stream of impossible situations and insoluble problems, not only for the individual, but for communities and nations. They do not fit into neat categories. So, in this chapter, we will provide five diversified examples of individual situations and problems, from real life, hypothetical, or a combination of both, and then show how to apply Autogenics for correction or solution. This will provide you with the basic how-to so you can apply Autogenics whenever it is needed in your life.

A Lagging Memory and How to Stimulate It

The original crooner, Rudy Vallee, was offered a part in a summer stock play, "How to Succeed in Business Without Really Trying." It was an opportunity for him to start a second career. After two rehearsals in which he muffed his lines, he was given an ultimatum: "Know your lines next rehearsal or else."

He came to us with very little time to do the job. The Mood, Relaxation, and Change Formulae were used. He practiced them several times. He restudied his part. He went on to become a success in that show and in future shows.

I am going to expand on this problem to include with memory the whole learning process so that it has value to all students, young and old.

Contrary to what most of us have been taught, learning comes easier and faster not when we try harder but when we relax.

The Lozonov method of Suggestology, now spreading beyond its Bulgarian origins to other countries including the United States, is a relaxed method of learning a foreign language. You sit in a comfortable stuffed chair and listen to symphonic music while the instructor intones the vocabulary. Without paying attention to him, you learn faster.

Any system of learning which uses relaxation and imagery is bound to be an improvement over standard nose-to-the-grindstone tension wrought methods.

So, in Autogenics, although six different suggestions or instructions are provided in the Change Formula, the most important is the first one given below, namely, you will be relaxed, calm, and composed while studying.

For the Mood Formula, you will need the black dot created in the last chapter—a piece of white paper with a black "bullseye" drawn on it. For the Relaxation Formula, you will again be given the choice of the lengthy tape or monologue used in earlier chapters, or a free-wheeling relaxation in which you employ the same techniques more informally—progressive relaxation, arm levitation, countdown, etc.

This free-wheeling relaxation can be your choice over the lengthy monologue from now on, especially if you have been through the tape or monologue a number of times.

For learning, here are the three formulae:

Mood Formula: Concentrate on a candle, or a spot on the wall or ceiling, and focus your attention on that point. Block out everything else about you. After a while imagine that your eyes are heavy and then let them close. Concentrate on a positive suggestion and then imagine yourself following through.

Relax, and close your eyes. Recite the addition tables: 1 + 1 = 2, 1 + 2 = 3, 1 + 3 = 4, etc. until 9 + 9 = 18.

Keep your attention focused on the mental task and notice when your mind wanders. Always bring yourself back to the task. After a few days, change to the multiplication table for variety.

Relaxation Formula: Formal or informal.

Change Formula:

I am relaxed, calm, and composed while studying (on the test, at the lecture).
I am deeply interested and involved in what I am doing.
I am able to concentrate without distractions or interruptions.
I can block out everything else about me.
What I start, I finish.
I can recall anything I learn.

Of course, you always end your Autogenics sessions with a count-up, giving yourself instructions on the way so that when you open your eyes you will be wide awake and feeling great.

How to Get More Done in the Limited Time Available

One of the most frustrating situations, creating problems that seem impossible to solve, is the one involving time. Typical examples are:

- Completing a report or paper that is due by a certain date.
- Meeting a sales or production goal by the end of the period.
- Getting everything done before a scheduled departure or a scheduled event.
- Doing what is required of your during the average day at home or on the job.
- Preparing for a meeting or appointment hours or minutes away.

Again, contrary to what we are probably doing in these situations now, relaxation is the key. The more we permit deadlines to cause tension, the more "dead" we become.

George was a go-getter. His life insurance sales were tops in the agency time after time. But time was running out for George. He had developed occasional chest pains and frequent tension headaches. His doctor advised slowing down and losing weight. He came to us for help in both. George used the Autogenics approaches in Chapter 7 for the weight loss and the following Autogenics approach for the pressure of time. When he came to the final visualization of the Change Formula, he saw himself relaxed about making calls—and making sales. Today, George is both healthier and wealthier.

To insure that your relaxation will not be too informal, I am going to recommend the tape or monologue, but will still give you the choice of using it or going a more free-wheeling route. However, if you choose to be informal, review the informal relaxation steps given below and use them as your informal Relaxation Formula.

Mood Formula: Use the two-path exercise. Relax and imagine you come to a fork in the path. On the left path, you never have enough time to meet a deadline. Life is one frustration after another; you see yourself tense and irritable; seldom do things go right and you wind up late—except for your death which, due to your stressed life, comes early.

But on the right-hand path, you see yourself relaxed about deadlines. You take time out for your Autogenics sessions. You get more done in less time and better. You are under no tension. You meet deadlines with time to spare. You are healthier and live longer. You choose and step off on the right-hand path.

Relaxation Formula:

Step One: Breathing. First become aware of your breathing as you breathe in and as you breathe out. Then take a few deep breaths. Remember to hold each breath and let the air out slowly, feeling the control you have over that breath. Then breathe quietly, gently and steadily, just the way you breathe when you are tired or when you are about to fall asleep. Imagine the feeling of drowsiness. Feel yourself drifting or floating.

Step Two: Progressive Relaxation. Relax all of your muscles. Let them go limp and slack. Feel your entire body as if it were like a heavy lead weight. Imagine each part of your body relaxed, starting from your feet and ankles, then into your calves and thighs, your abdomen and chest, down your shoulders, into your back, your arms, hands and fingers, neck, face. Even your mind is relaxed—no thoughts, worries, or problems.

Step Three: Imagined Scene. Imagine yourself on a beach, by a lake, in a meadow, floating on a cloud, making love, etc.

Step Four: Count Down. Count down from 10 to 1. Imagine you are relaxing deeper and deeper. You can go down stairs, elevators, or escalators.

Change Formula:

I am relaxed, calm and composed in any situation, regardless of the time factor.

I am aware of time but it is my friend.

I am able to relax away tension before it can build.

I am patient, understanding, and compassionate.

I am efficient and effective.

I see myself now completing what has to be done today (tomorrow, this week, etc.) with time to spare, relaxed and energetic. (Image the activities and the clock, seeing yourself relaxed and effective, completing ahead of time.)

Time is elastic. If you are aware of time, it goes by slowly. If you watch for the kettle to boil, it takes forever. Programming to be aware of time as your friend, without feeling pressured or intimidated by it, actually stretches time in terms of your ability to use it.

Knowing this you have every reason to be relaxed about time and this stretches time for you even more.

Kiss deadlines goodbye. They are now lifelines.

How to Become a Super-Charged Idea Generator

Kevin, 55, was a former navy fighter pilot who had made a success as an industrial designer specializing in kitchen design. He had reached a point where his creativity seemed to be blocked. He found he was too cautious, leaning toward the tried and true rather than innovating in a creative way to meet special situations. He felt this had halted his progress.

"I seem to be unable to move in a career direction more satisfying and remunerative," Kevin explained. He said that the more successful he had become, the more time-consuming paper work there was to do, the more he procrastinated with it, and the less time there was for ideating.

At our initial interview, I found Kevin pleasant and outgoing. He had a happy marriage. Of his nine children, six were on their own and three teenagers remained in the nest. I found no contributing factors at home, so we focused on his office situation.

Kevin went through the Autogenics procedures described in this section. He practiced at home several times a week. In four months, Kevin reported that his procrastination disappeared. He was less fearful and more optimistic. His approach to design problems became bolder and more original. As a result, he became happier about himself and more positive in his attitudes. His energy grew by leaps and bounds. He became more motivated. ''And I sleep better, too,'' he added.

You might not be an ex-navy pilot, but you might be a procrastinator. You might not be an industrial designer, but you might find it difficult to come up with new ideas. You might not be like Kevin in any way and yet find that you have the same shortage of energy and ambition.

Here, then, are the three formulae to apply:

Mood Formula: Sit with a pad and pencil or pen. You are about to enter into contract negotiations with yourself. You are going to define your goals; set the time it will take to reach them; state exactly how you will go about to reach them, and then sign your name. In Kevin's case, the contract looked like this:

Goal:	To procrastinate less with paperwork. To become more creative, a generator of ideas. To have more ambition.
Time:	Better and better every day. Substantial progress in four months.
How:	Through Autogenics and self-understanding.

Your Goal, Time, and How will be different from Kevin's. Write them down now. Sign your name at the bottom and write the date next to your signature. You have just made a contract with yourself and you are ready to relax.

Relaxation Formula: Use the informal procedure given in the previous section of this chapter.

Change Formula:

I have unlimited potential.
I look forward to life's challenges.
I am aware of life's opportunities.
I enjoy setting goals and the satisfaction of achieving them.
What I start, I finish, and I do so on schedule.
I live up to my contracts.
I am a limitless source of ideas.
I am creative, efficient and effective.

How to Win Control Over Others for Goal Reaching

Head colds are contagious. If you have a head cold and cough or sneeze in someone's proximity, that person can catch your cold if his or her level of resistance is low.

Success is contagious, too. Everybody is ready to jump aboard the success bandwagon, especially if their own success levels are low. The ''sneeze'' in this case is enthusiasm.

Enthusiasm is infectious. If you can ignite your own enthusiasm, you win others to your support.

The anatomy of enthusiasm can be quite complicated, especially in matters involving family, business, society, and politics. A cheerleader is enthusiastic. He or she goes through vocal and physical demonstrations of that enthusiasm. But here it is just a simple matter of being in favor of winning.

Enthusiasm in the game of life involves a number of attributes. All of them need to be reinforced in order for you to radiate the genuine enthusiasm that causes family, friends, co-workers or voters to flock to your support. Let me list 20 of the most important of these attributes:

- Positive mental attitude
- Definiteness of purpose
- Energy to spare

- Conviction of beliefs
- Idealistic goals
- Good physical and mental health
- Personal initiative
- Self-discipline
- Applied faith
- Willingness to go the extra mile
- Accurate, clear thinking
- Team work
- Creative vision
- Pleasing personality
- Controlled attention
- Empathy for all people
- Willingness to take responsibility
- Confidence in leadership ability
- Ability to communicate clearly
- Willingness to give freedom to others to make their own decision.

Let's examine how Robert was able to use these building blocks to create irresistible enthusiasm. A 41-year-old stockbroker, he was making a living but not much more. He had just gone through his second divorce when I saw him. He lived alone now in a small apartment in suburban New York. Because he had no friends, his main activity was reading *The Wall Street Journal* and a half dozen investment bulletins.

Recently, a neighbor had talked him into going to an encounter group. The minute he got there, he was sorry. He took a chair outside the half-circle formed by the 11 participants. He felt angry at having agreed to come to this uncomfortable session.

Within three or four minutes, the leader of the group, a bearded young man in jeans and turtleneck, looked directly at Robert and asked, "Well, who are you? What do you want?"

"Who am I, what do I want?" replied Robert. "My name is Robert. I want happiness. But I doubt a slob like you could solve my problems, or anybody else's for that matter."

The leader nodded and turned to another participant. "Why is Robert so angry?"

"I don't know," replied the other, "Maybe he is always angry."

Robert told me that incident right off. Obviously, it had thrown some light on why he did not convince his clients to buy his investment service, why he did not convince two wives of his adequacy as a husband, and why other people turned their backs on him leaving him friendless.

We agreed—and Robert's finger levitation test agreed—that substituting friendly enthusiasm for hostile anger should be his target. In the process of setting the mood, Robert kept thinking of his late father who was also always hostile and angry. For the first time, Robert realized he was being like his father instead of being like himself. That realization entered his Change Formula ("I am enthusiastic about being my own person"). But his Change Formula still included the building blocks listed above.

Within months the changes in Robert were dramatic. He had a roommate whom he planned to marry. He was a happy man. His client relations had improved. He was enthusiastic about the investment decisions he made and conveyed. He was named vice-president of the brokerage firm.

Home life and social life also respond to enthusiasm. Take the case of Margaret. When I saw her for the first time, she was in a terrible state. "I have no patience with my four boys and my husband is no help," she explained. She told me, "I am too tired to do anything. It is all just too much. I don't have time to take care of myself. I just can't go on."

Margaret went into more detail about her endless "picking up" after her husband and four boys. "Nobody picks up for me." I asked here about her neighbors and friends. Yes, she knew families with four children. "I just don't know how they do it," she said, "They must have more energy, more enthusiasm about their family."

Her target became "order" and "enthusiasm." She used the formulae described below, adding "order" to the Change Formula. The changes that took place in Margaret surprised even me. She became calm. She convinced her husband and children to perform more of their own chores. She developed outside interests. "I am overcoming obstacles that stood in my way," she told me over the phone. I didn't ask her to explain that, but then she said something that didn't require an explanation. "You know, I think I'm beginning to enjoy my family."

I am not going to ask you again to be enthusiastic about whipping up enthusiasm. I merely ask you to go through the Mood Formula, the Relaxation Formula, and the Change Formula that follow and to reinforce them every few days. Then you will have something to be enthusiastic about.

Mood Formula: Relax and daydream about the way things are. What key negative attitude in your life might be dampening your spirits, creating unhappiness, boredom, or despondency? Give it a name; i.e., impatience, intolerance, anger, hostility, etc. Now pick a word that is the opposite of this key negative attitude; i.e., patient instead of impatient, tolerant instead of intolerant, elated instead of angry, friendly instead of hostile. Put yourself in typical day-to-day scenes, as if you were on a stage. See yourself acting out this key negative attitude. See the curtain go down. See a large word on the curtain "AUTOGENICS." See the curtain go up. The scene has changed. You are now acting out the positive opposite. See yourself in typical day-to-day scenes, being positive, radiating enthusiasm to others.

Relaxation Formula: Your choice.

Change Formula: Pick the building blocks that contribute most to the positive opposite enjoyed in your Mood Formula. Put the words "I have ..." In front and mentally affirm at least five statements, as, "I have a positive mental attitude. I have definiteness of purpose. I have energy to spare." End by repeating the final act in your Mood Formula, seeing yourself surrounded by supportive people (in whatever area you need support) irresistibly attracted to you by your genuine enthusiasm.

Winning Consent from the Opposite Sex

The ability to engineer consent is at the core of public relations. It is also at the core of private relations.

As a result, success in business or in family or in society or in politics also goes hand in hand with success in love.

This chapter would not be complete without a reminder that, as you use Autogenics to enhance your control over other people through the attractive force of enthusiasm, you are bound to become more attractive to the opposite sex. This means less resistance to your invitations, advances, proposals and propositions.

It happens naturally, without my specific Change Formula directed at the opposite sex. It happens when your Change Formula is directed at the positive building blocks for enthusiasm listed earlier in this chapter.

Why? It centers on life energy. Nobody is attracted to a half-dead person, whether half-dead physically, mentally, or spiritually. When such a person comes to life, eyes turn in his direction. Anything you do to set up your own voltage, will step up your sexual attractiveness. What is voltage? Enthusiasm.

Rosalyn was forty years old. She had been divorced for the past five years and lived with her nineteen-year-old son. Her problem was that she did not think that she was good at anything. She considered herself a failure as a wife and a failure as a mother. She also felt that she was unattractive (although she was not) and that she was overweight (which she was not). In an attempt to establish new relationships, she had gone through the "singles scene" but felt awkward about speaking to strangers and felt out of place in the singles world. As far as she was concerned, her life was at an end. Although she wasn't suicidal, she was despondent and wholly negative.

She was not in need financially. Her ex-husband, an attorney, had provided well for her in the divorce settlement.

It was difficult to establish Rosalyn's goal. She was listless and unambitious. Most of her thoughts were of anger and hostility about the wasted years of her life. She kept harping on the fact that she was unsuccessful. For a while we talked about the qualities of successful people and she began to become interested. We generally agreed that a person can be unsuccessful, but an unsuccessful person can become successful. She conceded that if she were to feel successful, that most of her feelings of depression would be relieved.

We discussed one aspect of successful people: they exhaust every plausible avenue. She agreed she had not begun to seek successful directions. In any case, we had established our primary goal—"success." I informed Rosalyn that, in my opinion, she had unsuccessful beliefs about herself being fed to her by her subconscious. Her mind presently believed that she was a failure and that was the message being fed to her, and that the pathway her mind had been taking for years always ended at a negative point. Now we were going to take a new pathway. Our target point was "success."

Rosalyn went through the procedure just outlined to control others, emphasizing positive statements for success—success in business and success in attracting men—both factors went hand in hand in her concept of a success life.

Within weeks, Rosalyn reported to me that she had more energy and more drive—and more men friends. She took over a small boutique store on Long Island's North Shore. It was doing quite well. Since she lived with her teenage son, the store became her trysting place after hours. Success in business and success in love were going hand in hand.

Mood Formula: Same as under "How to Win Control Over Others in Goal Reaching."

Relaxation Formula: Your choice.

Change Formula: Again, the same as under controlling others.

CHAPTER 12

Acquiring a Winning Personality

THE KEY TO AUTOGENICS IS CHANGE. The mood is set. The relaxation makes change possible. The formula for change is applied. And it is done. The mind has been programmed to respond, to think, to make you feel different.

The change is always for the better. The change is always from the unwanted to the wanted, from the unattainable to the attainable, from negative to positive, from "I can't" to "I can."

Note that there are always opposites involved. We turn from being poor at something to being good at something, from being a loser to being a winner, from failure to success.

Yes, there are factors such as old conditionings that need to be addressed, such as readiness to create a change, such as belief that a change is possible. We addressed those factors in earlier chapters of this book.

Now that you are able to test for the existence of those factors and to handle them if they are present, the only instruction left for me to provide you with is the instruction for reversing the unwanted to the wanted.

In the last chapter, you created opposites as your Change Formula and in previous chapters, you were supplied with opposites to use in Change Formula.

Adopting the opposite of what you do not want to continue is a Universal Change Formula.

In this chapter, we will close the instruction in Autogenics by giving you simplified Mood, Relaxation, and Change Formulae that can be used universally for all matters that arise which are not covered in this book.

"Today something is happening to the structure of human consciousness," wrote Teilhard de Chardin, "A fresh kind of life is starting." That fresh kind of life is the opposite of the stale kind of life.

You might move from putting people down to putting up with people. You might move from a life of hate and destruction to a life of love and creativity. You might move from annoyance and despondency to peace and joy.

You are doing an "about face." We turn from negative to positive. The negative inhibits and blocks happiness. The positive calls forth the best from within us and creates happiness.

Autogenics for a Mental "About-Face"

If you found yourself prone to making verbal blunders such as unintended insults or in other ways "putting your foot in your mouth" what Change Formula would you use to do a verbal about-face? Think about it. I'll give you an answer in a moment.

If you found yourself prone to criticizing others, belittling their suggestions, and in other ways putting them down, what Change Formula would you use to turn that trait from negative to positive?

If you found yourself prone to thinking in terms of "I can't" instead of "I can," and, as a result, you were not even setting goals for fear of not reaching them, what Change Formula would you use to give yourself a kick in the "can'ts"?

Think about all three and come up with a suggested statement to use while relaxed.

"Keep your face to the sunshine and you cannot see the shadow," said Helen Keller who, as you know, was blind. About-face.

Here are three about-face statements that apply in the above three cases. See how they compare with your statements.

If you are always putting your foot in your mouth: "I always say the right thing at the right time."

If you are over-critical of others: "I am loving, understanding and compassionate. I call forth the best in myself and others."

If you habitually think you can't: "I am capable, efficient and effective. Obstacles stimulate my resourcefulness. I rise above self-conceived limits and am able to do more and more."

If you came up with similar statements, then you successfully completed an about-face. Perhaps your statements did not go as far. Then you need to re-examine them and see how they can be revised to make them reflect more of that opposite direction.

How to Stop Putting Your Foot in Your Mouth

Once you have your statement, you have your Mood Formula and your Change Formula. For example:

Mood Formula (putting your foot in your mouth): Remember the last time or a specific time when you said the wrong thing. Recall the embarrassment or chagrin. Now imagine your saying the right thing at that time. Notice how differently you feel.

Relaxation Formula: Your favorite way.

Change Formula: Repeat mentally a few times:

"I always say the right thing at the right time."

Now spend a minute or two daydreaming about the changes that are now going to take place as a result of this about-face—the increase in friends, more appreciation by superiors, improvement in personal relationships. End with the usual count-up.

Doing an About-Face on a Critical Attitude

Mood Formula (over-critical of others): Review one of your biggest put-downs. Remember how you felt when you did it, as if by putting down that person you were boosting yourself, but how the end result was really a letdown for you. Now imagine praising that person instead. It may seem hard to do. But do it in your imagination. "See" that person reacting with gratitude and appreciation, returning the compliment or praising you at the first opportunity. How does it feel?

Relaxation Formula: Your favorite way.

Change Formula: Repeat mentally a few times:

"I am loving, understanding and compassionate. I call forth the best in myself and in others."

Now daydream a minute or two about the changes that are going to take place in your spouse, your partner, your neighbor, or other inter-personal relationships and how the changes in them will make changes for the better in your life. See yourself being supportive and supported. End with the usual count-up.

Going from "I Can't" to "I Can"

Mood Formula (''I can't''): Review a past incident where you refused to try. Remember your attitude at that time, including your lack of security and possible feelings of inferiority. Now imagine you said ''I can'' and proceeded to try. Imagine your doing whatever was necessary to see it through successfully. How does it feel when you finally accomplish your goal?

Relaxation Formula: Your favorite way.

Change Formula: Repeat mentally a few times:

> *''I am capable, efficient, and effective. Obstacles stimulate my resourcefulness. I rise above self-conceived limits and am able to do more and more.''*

Now select a situation that is intimidating today. See yourself changing from the tendency to avoid it, or circumvent it, or back off from it, and instead confronting it with confidence and diligence. You handle it successfully. End with the usual count-up.

Changing Your Traits from Liabilities to Assets

You can do as many about-faces as there are defects in your personality, weaknesses in your character, and unwanted aspects to your behavior.

Using the three examples for which I have just given you the formulae, you can create a Change Formula based on the opposite of your unwanted trait. Here are 25 more traits and their about-face counterparts. Note which ones you might have. They are your liabilities. Note their opposites. Program for these and you will have fewer liabilities and more assets.

That means you will have a greater net worth.

These negative liabilities	can be changed to	*These positive assets*
Emotional		Stable
Rigid		Adaptable
Jealous		Trusting
Friendless		Popular
Lonely		Busy
Feelings of worthlessness		Feelings of self-worth
Poor speaker		Good conversationalist
Worrier		Optimist
Non-doer		Doer
Failure-prone		Success-prone
Grieving		Cheerful
Nervous		Relaxed
Tense		Calm
Weak-willed		Strong-willed
Indecisive		Decisive
Sad		Joyous
Loner		Outgoing
Destructive		Constructive
Unimaginative		Creative
Apprehensive		Confident
Self-guilt		Self-acceptance
Confined		Free
Afraid		Courageous
Lazy		Energetic
Apathetic		Ambitious

Proper Autogenics Approaches for Deeply Rooted Problems

When Margaret's husband left her and moved in with a girl friend 15 years younger than Margaret's 38 years, she went into complete withdrawal. She gave up her interest in shopping, gardening, ceramics and her children's school activities. She never left the house. She hardly ever left her bed. Margaret had developed agoraphobia—a fear of going anywhere where there are open, public places.

After two physicians, a mental health clinic, three psychiatrists, two hospital stays and a chiropractor had failed to help her, Margaret came to us.

We helped Margaret understand the root of her problem. We helped her check her subconscious readiness to face that problem. In other words, we guided Margaret through a Mood Formula designed to identify her target and helped her with finger levitation in order to determine her readiness for change. These are the procedures given you in the first half of this book.

They may work for you without professional help. I certainly hope so. I doubt if they would have for Margaret, considering her lack of willingness to do anything, especially something so novel. My point is that some problems do not respond to a simple attempt to make an about-face. They need to be pulled out by the roots.

With our help, Margaret did exactly that. Within six months, she was able to take walks with her dog, drive the car locally and go shopping. She would go to a movie but insist on sitting near an exit and she would still not go to parties or take long trips. But life was improving for Margaret as she continued to relax daily and go through her visual imaging to improve still further. She was returning to her "easy going, fun-loving self again."

Now Angela's problem was the same as Margaret's but not quite as pronounced. Also in her late thirties, Angela could not put her finger on any one time or incident when she began to feel uneasy about taking even local trips or staying away from her apartment overnight. One factor that was similar to Margaret's: Angela's marriage was in her own terms a zero. Zero compatability, zero support, zero companionship. Angela sold supplies to optometrists and her problem was jeopardizing her job.

Angela was excellent in her relaxation and imaging. She was also quite motivated compared to Margaret. We turned the major therapeutic role back to her. We gave her initial Autogenic experiences and she agreed to practice daily.

We checked on Angela nine months later. We could tell just a few seconds into the phone conversation that this was a success story—she was communicative and enthusiastic. She reported she was still relaxing daily and imaging positively. She had more confidence and energy and was able to take short trips away from home, as required by her work, with no trepidation.

The root of Angela's problem was not as deep as Margaret's. It did not take as much professional skill. She could handle it herself with initial guidance. Had this book been written, Angela could probably have used it: not so Margaret. She would still need professional help.

Another brief case history: Patricia, 34, a housewife received no pleasure from the sexual act. Her husband was considerate and patient, but he, too, was frustrated by her inability to have an orgasm. We saw Patricia as a motivated client with a good understanding of her problem. She had been up-tight about having sexual relations as a newlywed 14 years before, and this tenseness had never left her. Of course, the more she tried now to have a climax, the more tense she became. It was a "vicious cycle."

Patricia was able to break that cycle. The key was relaxation. She needed only minor instructions with that. The Change Formula was based on two clues: One, she had had a strict Victorian-type upbringing that gave sex a bad name. Two, she was afraid of being hurt during her first sexual experience. So the Change Formula included these two about-faces. One: "It is perfectly normal, moral, and healthy to let go and experience pleasure." Two, "Nothing will hurt me. I am able to let go."

No, there was no need of "I will climax." Patricia had to merely get out of her own way by giving up her controls.

Patricia did it all by herself. Now, a year later, she climaxes like any normal woman. She gets a pleasure that she never got before from each aspect of foreplay and coitus. She still occasionally uses her Autogenics to raise her sexual sensitivity even more.

There are all degrees of problems. We have placed the more difficult ones in the first half of this book. They are not usually responsive to the simple about-face procedures we are now discussing in this final chapter. In fact, it could be dangerous to try. You might set up mental conflicts which would only complicate the problem.

However, if you feel your situation is more of a trait you would like to replace than a problem you would like to uproot, the simple procedure of setting the mood by identifying the trait, relaxing, and giving about-face instructions for change is bound to be effective.

A Change Formula to Explode Abounding Success

I wish I knew who wrote this—I would give him or her credit rightly due:

> If you think you are beaten, you are.
> If you think you dare not, you don't.
> If you'd like to win, but think you can't,
> it's almost a cinch you won't.
> If you think you'll lose, you're lost.
> For out in the world we find
> Success begins with a fellow's will:
> It's all in the state of mind.
> Life's battles don't always go
> to the stronger or faster man.
> But sooner or later the man who wins
> is the one who thinks he can.

You can succeed.

You can set goals and reach them.

Many individuals have clearly defined goals. At this specific point in time they know exactly what direction to go in order to be just where they want to be by another specific point in time.

For these individuals, specific Mood and Change Formulae are constructed to program successful goal reaching.

For other individuals, goals are more general. In matters of income, say, they would merely like to have more leeway. In matters of family, perhaps they would like more leisure time to spend with spouse and children. In social matters, they would like to get along better with people. In spiritual matters, more peace of mind. In mental ability, more awareness and recall. In attitude, more optimism and feeling "up."

Where goals are general and perhaps more scattered, you can use the "shot gun" approach in Autogenics. You can use a "Change Formula" that touches all the bases.

I am going to give you such a Change Formula. Because it covers a lot of ground, it must be repeated on a daily schedule for a period of time in order for its effects in specific areas to be noticed.

However, it is a powerful antidote for failure, gloomy attitudes, and apathy. It can spark an energy explosion within you. It can touch off creative ability you never realized you had. It can move you to higher and higher peaks of success.

Here is the procedure.

Mood Formula: Use the two-path exercise. See yourself as you are now, on the left-hand path. Note the dissatisfaction with certain departments of your life. Look up the right-hand path. See yourself doing Autogenics. See improvements in skills, attitudes, and traits. See the resulting benefits in certain departments of your life. Make the decision as to which path you wish to take. See yourself stepping off on that path.

Relaxation Formula: The best thing to do is to use the lengthy tape. Having the long monologue read by another person would be excellent, too, but you might be deterred from making this a daily event if you have to impose on somebody. If you have not made a relaxation tape based on the monologue in Chapter 3, you might want to consider doing it now because you will probably use a tape for your Change Formula. But rather than delay or procrastinate, I would settle for your relaxing deeply using whatever methodology you were comfortable with in previous chapters— the progressive muscle relaxation, the hand levitation, the countdowns, the tranquil scenes.

Change Formula: Here is where you will need a tape. A cooperative person willing to work with you daily is the only alternative. The tape will take about five minutes. When combined with the time needed for setting the mood, and for relaxing with the relaxation tape, you will be investing about 15 minutes a day in your forthcoming success.

Here is the material to be read or taped. Read it through now.

Is there any part you feel you must reject? Then examine the trait that is blocking you and do a special Autogenics session to do an about-face on that trait.

On the other hand, if you can accept the programming, you are ready to use it.

> "I acquire knowledge and find ways to use it. I put forth my best efforts at all times. I have faith in myself to do that which is right. I am confident in my physical strength and my mental ability. I am energetic. I am true to myself and to others. My conduct is at the highest level of responsibility to myself and to my fellow man. I work for my good and for the good of mankind. I do everything to the best of my ability and I improve in this ability each time I use it.
>
> "I use my increased abilities to help myself and my fellow man. I see good in all people and in all events. I dwell on the positive effects. In all my relationships, I forgive others for their negativity, and I forgive myself. I participate in no negative gossip or judgments. When I speak I emphasize what is kind, truthful and supportive.
>
> "I grow mentally and spiritually every day. I am able to govern my affairs with maturity and wisdom. I act with discipline, energy and order. I am in harmony with the laws of society, business, and nature. These words are perfecting my behavior, releasing me from false limitations and restoring my full potential. My senses are becoming more acute. I see better. I hear better. My sense of taste, smell and touch are more sensitive. My relaxation is permitting my glands, organs, and nerves to function rhythmically and in balance. I gain perfect health. My youthfulness and vitality are enhanced. My harmony within is manifested in every cell of my body. This harmony is reflected in my family relationships, my business, and my social life. I enjoy great power and prosperity. Infinite energy and abundance are mine to harness to fill my needs. I am rich in gratitude, empathy and love for people generally and the persons I live and work with specifically.
>
> "I am in control of my mind at all times, in control of my attention, my moods and my personality. I use that control to prevent the negative and promote the positive toward my sound physical and mental health and toward harmony with others. I am solution-oriented. I think accurately and logically when

needed. I think intuitively and creatively when needed. I am able to coordinate both types of thinking when needed.

"I plan my day and work my plan. I am organized and efficient. I am able to concentrate without letting distractions interfere. I make decisions based on available options and the best chances for success in reaching my goal. I am able to evaluate results and set progressive goals. I make the most of each day.

"I awake each morning rested and refreshed, energetic and enthusiastic. I am becoming a more dynamic, productive and self-reliant person with each successive day. I set an example for others. I am a doer. I am a giver. I am an achiever.

"Daily I am more and more successful. I become my highest self."

Count yourself up at the end of the tape feeling wide awake and rarin' to go.

It has been a pleasure sharing Autogenics with you. I know that that pleasure will also be yours.

APPENDIX

THIS IS AN OPTIONAL TAPE or monologue to use for weight loss. It combines the Relaxation Formula and Change Formula. Use the Mood Formula given in Chapter 7, then listen to the following:

Now I want you to make yourself comfortable. Prepare yourself to relax. In a moment I will ask you to take three deep breaths and, as you exhale on the third breath, I will ask you to then to close your eyes. So now take your first deep breath and prepare your mind and your body to relax. Now take your second breath. Make it a deep breath. As you exhale, relax a little more. And now take your third breath and, as you exhale, will you please close your eyes. Comfortably close your eyes. You will keep your eyes closed until I tell you to open them. As you sit there relaxing and listening to my voice and following my instructions, you will soon find that you are relaxing more and more deeply. You will find that you are relaxing deeper and deeper, drifting down further and further into a very deeply relaxed state. Now when I say the word limp, I want you to immediately allow all the muscles in your body to become limp, to become soft and slack, limp like a rag doll. Let them go limp now, become aware of the slackness in your muscles as you let the muscles become limp. Become aware of the feeling of relaxation, restful, soothing and quiet. Now I am going to ask you to relax each part of your body. Begin with your feet and your ankles. Let the muscles of your feet and ankles relax. Just let them go limp. Now let the muscles of your legs go limp and slack and as they relax more and more, begin to feel the growing sensation of heaviness in your feet and in your legs. And the limper you allow your feet and your legs to become, the more relaxed they will become, the heavier they will feel and soon the feeling of relaxed limp heaviness drifts into your calves, into your thighs, you feel the sensations of relaxation and you feel the tensions just draining away as you relax more and more. And you also begin to notice a feeling of comfort and security as the feeling of limp heaviness spreads through your whole body and relaxes it deeper and deeper. You feel all the tension just draining away.

And this wonderful feeling of tranquility and relaxation spreads and extends into the muscles of your abdomen, into your chest and you begin to feel your whole body becoming loose and limp, and all the tensions just drifting away, just draining away. The feelings of relaxation are flowing through your body, flowing from your feet into your thighs and into your abdomen, flowing and drifting into your chest, into your shoulders, looser and limper as you drift down into a comfortable, pleasant relaxed tranquility. The relaxation and limpness that flow over your shoulders continue to drift down through your back and the remaining tensions drain away. And you can let yourself go completely, you can totally permit yourself to drift down deeper and deeper, and the slackness and looseness can continue to totally relax you. Feel the flow of this wonderful feeling continuing, continuing into the muscles of your neck, and all the muscles in the front of your neck, the side of your neck becoming looser and limper, just letting go, and finally you can relax the muscles in your face and in your cheeks. Let the muscles relax totally and completely, and as you continue with these feelings of relaxation, you will notice that you are beginning to feel the warmth and the heaviness that I told you that you would feel, and you can now give yourself over completely to these pleasant, comfortable sensations. Your breathing has become deep and regular, and your whole body has become totally and completely quiet, still and comfortable. Listen to what I say, just listen to my voice. You do not have to concentrate intensely. All you need to do is to listen and experience the feeling that I suggest, and then all the suggestions I will give you will have the effect that you want them to have. The feelings of relaxation that you are now experiencing are so pleasant to you; they are so pleasant that you do not wish to disturb them. They make you comfortable; so comfortable in fact, that you have no desire to move. You feel perfectly content just as you are. You can enjoy the feelings of being relaxed; nothing else will bother you, and although you are relaxing deeper and deeper now, you will notice that you can still be aware of everything that is around you. You will also find that you can disregard anything that you wish to disregard, yet pay attention to anything that you wish to pay attention to. Now I want you to realize that you are truly experiencing the feelings that I told you you would experience. Remember, at the beginning, I asked you to take three deep breaths and to close your eyes, and to relax your body, and I told you that you would become relaxed and you became relaxed. And now I tell you that although you are relaxed, it is possible to become even more deeply relaxed; much more deeply relaxed than you are now. And a doorway to much deeper relaxation is right in front of you now. Soon I will take you through this doorway into a much deeper state of relaxation, and when you reach that depth, I will make the suggestion to you that will cause you to achieve the very things that you wish to achieve. So now visualize the doorway. Now begin to open the door and, as you open it, I want you to see what is beyond it. For, behind the door there is a long, comfortable staircase, winding down and down. In the dim light, you are going to comfortably and safely begin to go down the staircase, eager to experience the feelings of deep relaxation that you will have as you go down each step. Now begin to descend down, slowly, one step after the other; step by step, going down deeper and deeper, step by step, more and more comfortable; deeper and deeper, slowly one step after the other, step by step; going down deeper and deeper, much more comfortable; deeper and deeper until finally, you reach the bottom of the staircase. And at the bottom, there is a platform, a platform that seems to be soft and comfortable, a platform like a deep couch, covered with soft cushions; and you're able to lie back on this couch and feel yourself sinking down into its softness. As you do, it gradually begins to drift slowly, as if it were floating, just floating and drifting. And you become aware of the whole feeling of the movement, the warmth, the comfort and the drowsiness as you keep drifting and drifting; and as you drift, you remember that when you were walking down the staircase, you were really going into a deeper and deeper state, so as to be able to respond to the suggestions that I am going to give you. And that each step really represented a deeper state of response, so when you reached the bottom, you were in as deep a state as you needed to be, as deep a state as necessary to respond to the suggestions, the suggestions that I am going to give you. These suggestions will take hold quickly and easily. Your mind will make use of the suggestions automatically whenever you need them. They will make the changes that will bring you total and absolute success, because from now on, you will have a new respect for your body, and a new respect for your health and your appearance. The old compulsive eating habits that you used to have are no longer present. You will have no impulse to overeat, you will have no more sudden urges to eat between meals; you will no longer have the habit of overeating. It will make no difference whether your habits were to overeat or to eat between meals, to eat in the evening or late at night; every habit that you ever had that encouraged you to overeat, that caused you to eat the wrong foods, will no longer be there. The old negative image that you used to have of yourself, of being out of control, is now replaced by a positive image of yourself in which you are healthy, vital and in control. Any of the old impulses or nervous eating habits that you had are now erased and wiped away. The compulsion to overeat is now replaced by a new awareness of yourself. You will never again reach for something to eat without thinking. You will not eat simply because you have nothing better to do. You will not eat simply because at that moment you happen to feel nervous or tense or bored; for, whatever reason in the past that caused you to act in that way, that reason is now gone, that reason is no longer valid. So whatever illogical beliefs you had that food could solve your problems or your boredom or your frustrations or your nervousness, those illogical beliefs have now gone. You totally and absolutely accept now that food cannot solve those problems or end boredom or deal with frustrations or offer any escape whatsoever. You can totally accept that now you will be able to deal with life's problems separately, in a more logical manner. From now on, each meal that you complete will completely satisfy your hunger and your appetite until it is time for your next regular meal. You will no longer act as you have in the past; from now on you will be in complete charge of your body, you will do only what is good for your body. Whatever reasons you had in the past for overeating, these reasons are insignificant now. They need no longer rule or effect your life in any way. As you listen to my voice, you feel your ego strengthening, becoming stronger and stronger. You feel your determination to take charge of yourself becoming stronger and stronger. From now on, you will do only those things that are good for your body. Your subconscious mind will now regulate your food needs intelligently and judge the correct type of foods and the correct amounts of foods so that anything more than moderate amounts of healthy foods will make you feel too full. You will never want to eat more than moderate amounts of healthy foods. Fattening foods are now ugly to you and no longer appeal to you. Any old habits that you had, habits that made you overweight, whether those habits were sneaking food or cheating in some manner, whatever those habits were, they are now all in the past because from now on you will only eat moderate amounts of food. You will get much more satisfaction out of being in charge of yourself, out of doing well, out of developing a healthy, slender body than you ever got from overeating. Each day you will have new self-confidence and a new ability, not only to lose weight, but to stay in charge of yourself. From now on you are going to be wonderfully positive and assertive. You are going to be able to lose all the weight that you desire to lose, and you will know that after you reach the weight that you want to reach, you will be able to maintain that weight. Every day your attitude will always be in the present, a day at a time, an hour at a time, a minute at a time. You will feel strong and complete. You will need no other crutch to reduce and maintain your slenderness because your subconscious mind will automatically respond by remembering all of the disagreeable aspects of being overweight. It will also remember all of the wonderful virtues of being healthy and slender. Each time you find yourself resisting food that you are not supposed to eat, you will immediately feel the rewards of that resistance. You will feel happy and proud of yourself. You will feel the feeling of confidence in your ability to control your life, to control what you eat. Each time you resist foods that you are not supposed to eat, you will immediately congratulate yourself, for your subconscious mind now has the ability to control what you eat, when to eat and to cause all of the loss of weight that you need to lose. You now have so much confidence and ability that once you have lost the weight, you will surely not gain it back. Now see yourself with the weight that you want to be, picture yourself firmly and clearly at the weight that you want to be, picture yourself firmly and clearly at the weight that you want to, and accept proudly and realistically that you will be that weight because, from now on, everything will be easier for you. You will find it easier to relax; you will no longer become as easily upset; you will no longer become as easily tense or anxious. I will tell you now how you will be able to control any sense of nervousness, to control it automatically; to control any sense of anxiety or tenseness or any impulse to overeat or overindulge. The way you will do it is, first, you will stop anything that you are doing. Just stop what you are doing. Next, you will take a single, deep breath, you will breathe in and slowly exhale. Let me repeat that instruction. First, you will stop what you are doing. Then, you will take a single, deep breath and slowly exhale. This single, deep breath will automatically relax you. Your nervousness will quickly dissipate. You will click back into being in charge of yourself, consciously and subconsciously. So now, with the absolute security of total success, once again visualize yourself at the weight that you want to be, and that is the weight that you will be, for now you have the capacity and the ability to lose every pound that you need to lose. The forces that caused you to overeat no longer control you. You are beyond those temptations. You are calm and relaxed; and you have the method now of taking charge of yourself and keeping in charge of yourself, and being in absolute and total control. Now in a few moments, we are going to return upward on that same staircase. And as we return upward, you are going to feel yourself becoming more and more wide awake; more and more alert, both mentally and physically. So now we come to the last five steps and when we get to the top step, you will open your eyes and feel wonderfully refreshed. Now, one, drifting higher and higher to a very normal wakefulness. Two, with wonderful, positive feelings. Three, higher and higher. Four, wider and wider awake. Five, feeling delightfully refreshed now. Open your eyes, feeling wonderful."

INDEX

R

S